The Three Porcupine Ridge

Jean M. Thompson

Alpha Editions

This edition published in 2023

ISBN : 9789357947701

Design and Setting By
Alpha Editions
www.alphaedis.com
Email - info@alphaedis.com

As per information held with us this book is in Public Domain.
This book is a reproduction of an important historical work. Alpha Editions uses the best technology to reproduce historical work in the same manner it was first published to preserve its original nature. Any marks or number seen are left intentionally to preserve its true form.

Contents

I	- 1 -
II RING NECK, LEADER OF THE FLYING WEDGE	- 5 -
III THE REVOLT OF TIMOTHY	- 10 -
IV THE LITTLE RED DOE OF DEER PASS	- 13 -
V DAME WOODCHUCK AND THE RED MONSTER	- 18 -
VI TRACKED BY A CATAMOUNT	- 22 -
VII THE CALL OF THE MOOSE	- 29 -
VIII THE LAST WOLF OF THE PACK	- 34 -
IX HOW UNK-WUNK THE PORCUPINE MET HIS MATCH	- 38 -
X THE GHOST OF THE WAINSCOT	- 43 -
XI WHY THE WEASEL NEVER SLEEPS	- 48 -
XII MRS. WHITE-SPOT AND HER KITTENS	- 52 -
XIII IN THE BOBCAT'S DEN	- 58 -
XIV WHY AHMUK THE BEAVER MOVED	- 64 -
XV NICODEMUS, KING OF CROW COLONY	- 69 -
XVI THE STORY OF RUSTY STARLING	- 74 -
XVII WHERE THE PARTRIDGE DRUMS	- 78 -
XVIII HOW SOLOMON OWL BECAME WISE	- 83 -
XIX THE KING OF BALSAM SWAMP	- 88 -
XX THE GIANT OF THE CORN-FIELD	- 93 -
XXI THE BRAVERY OF EBENEZER COON	- 99 -
XXII THE NARROW ESCAPE OF VELVET WINGS	- 103 -
XXIII NEMOX, THE CRAFTY ROBBER OF THE MARSHES	- 108 -
XXIV THE KEEPER OF TAMARACK RIDGE	- 113 -

I

THE THREE BEARS OF PORCUPINE RIDGE

"WOOF, woof, woof," called the little black mother bear gruffly, turning over a rotten log with her snout and uncovering a fine ant's nest.

"Woof, woof," answered back the two round black balls of animated fur—the cubs, as they scrambled eagerly and clumsily over the log, and began to feed greedily upon their mother's find.

The little black mother bear and her two cubs lived in a cozy den just below Porcupine Ridge, which happened to be far up on the side of Cushman Mountain. They were a happy little family, the three bears, and every day the two cubs grew more ball-like and lovable to their patient mother, who always managed to lead them to the very best feeding places. Through the dense, dark spruce forests, far down into the swamps below she took them, where they fed happily upon young frogs or crawfish, and the juicy sprouts of the skunk cabbages. Occasionally she would show them the way across the burnt swale, where the wild raspberries grew luscious and red.

The three bears nearly always slept inside their den the greater part of the day, but as soon as the hermit thrush began to sing her sleepy lullaby song, and the old gray hoot owl, who lived in a giant sycamore tree just below the Ridge, "who-oo, oo'd," then Mrs. Bear would nudge the two sleeping cubs with her snout, and cuff them about with her great paws playfully, until they were wide awake. Then off they would all three start in the moonlight to make a night of it in the forest. And they never thought of coming back to the den again until morning, when they had usually satisfied their pressing hunger.

Oh, life on Porcupine Ridge was peaceful and happy enough for the old mother bear and her two roly-poly cubs, and they were very contented with life until one eventful day something happened which changed everything, and this was how it came about.

One night, when it was "dark o' the moon," Mrs. Bear discovered a great patch of ripe raspberries in the edge of the swamp, and so while the two cubs were busy feeding upon the luscious berries, she suddenly became possessed with a keen desire for an adventure. So plunging deep into the swamp, she was soon across its treacherous quagmires, on through the dense spruce bush, and soon came out upon the far side of the swamp. She headed for the sheep pasture at first, but soon lost all desire for fresh lamb, for just then her keen nose had scented something far more desirable and delicious. It was honey.

On and on scrambled Mrs. Bear through the sheep pasture, utterly forgetting the cubs; past the rail fence she waddled, where sat the old gobbler turkey and his ten timorous wives, fast asleep, but uttering little, flurried peepings even in their dreams. But Mrs. Bear passed them carelessly by, and hurried on, with little eager "woof, woof's," until she had come to the farmer's home lot, and then she knew she had found that for which she searched, for suddenly she came upon five beehives. With her snout she soon managed to upset one hive, and then coat, snout and paws were soon smeared thickly with the sticky honey. Mrs. Bear might have wished the cubs were there, but if she did she was enjoying herself far too keenly to trouble about them then.

She soon finished one hive of honey and then turned over another, but as by this time she began to feel that she had had plenty for a while, just out of pure mischief, with her snout and paws, she simply tipped over the other hives. Suddenly Mrs. Bear discovered that a few angry bees had awakened and were clinging tightly to her thick fur, whereupon she immediately started off for the swamp at a quick, shambling trot, for well she remembered a certain deep, muddy water-hole, and making straight for the spot, she was soon rolling and wallowing contentedly about, trying to rid herself of the troublesome bees, and the sticky honey. It was here that the cubs joined their mother, who grunted and "woof, woofed," and as soon as the long yellow rays of approaching dawn began to shoot up from the other side of the mountain, the three bears scrambled back to their den on the Ridge, and were soon fast asleep.

Of course the farmer found his overturned beehives, the next morning, and angry enough he was, I can tell you.

"Ugh, a bear did this," he grumbled, as he examined closely the great, wide footprints which Mrs. Bear had left all over the ground. By following the bear tracks the farmer soon knew just what ground the old bear had covered. He even traced her to the mud wallow where she had rid herself of the bees and honey. Then the farmer sat about concocting a scheme to catch Mrs. Bear, for well he knew she would return again after more honey. But if there is one thing in all the world which a bear enjoys eating more than honey, it is a great hunk of crumbly maple sugar, for bears have a wonderfully keen sweet tooth. The farmer climbed up Mount Cushman, and when he had reached a spot in the very heart of the spruce woods, which happened to be about a mile below Porcupine Ridge, he went to work and set a trap for Mrs. Bear, and this is how he went about it.

First he hollowed out a kind of den near a deep spring, around which grew quantities of jack-in-the-pulpit plants, for the bears dearly love to browse upon the tender shoots of these plants. Then in the hollow he placed the bear trap, made of strong steel. After setting the trap he covered it craftily over with a layer of loose twigs, upon which he put, last of all, a great piece of soft, springy moss. Back of the trap he laid the bait temptingly, which happened to be a dead woodchuck. So that when Mrs. Bear should step upon the moss tussock covering the steel trap, she would instantly spring it.

Then the farmer went home and waited, visiting the trap daily, to see if Mrs. Bear had been there. Of course she had visited the place, for there the farmer found bear tracks, but who cares for a dead woodchuck when the blackberries are ripe, the frogs young and tender, and there is even honey, if one cares to go a journey for it.

At last the farmer was almost in despair, thinking old Mrs. Bear never would be caught, and he knew when food grew scarce in winter time his turkeys and young lambs would no longer be safe from Mrs. Bear. So finally he thought out a new plan. And that very night when Mrs. Bear and the two cubs halted at the spring on their way down from the Ridge, to munch jack-in-the-pulpit sprouts, Mrs. Bear paused and stuck her black snout inquisitively inside the farmer's den, and what do you suppose met her astonished eyes? Right over back of the moss tussock which concealed the trap, instead of the dead woodchuck was a great, brown hunk of hard maple sugar. Mrs. Bear would travel far for honey, but she completely lost her head when she scented maple sugar, so she planted one great, padded foot in the center of the moss tussock, then, before she knew it, something stung and gripped like fire into her great fore-paw, and with a sudden howl of surprise and rage, she backed out of the den, trying with all her might to shake off the cruel, biting thing which hurt her foot so wretchedly.

Meantime, the cubs sat up in amazement among the tall ferns, and looking at their mother's sad plight, howled and whined in sympathy.

Quite mad by this time with her agony and rage, not knowing what she was about, Mrs. Bear bolted, with the trap still clinging to her foot. Cutting a great, wide path in her flight through the underbrush on she ran. Up and down the mountain she tore, all night long, with the cruel trap ever biting deeper and deeper into her foot at every turn.

"Bang, bang," went the farmer's gun, and the cubs hearing the loud noise, terrified out of their small wits, scurried off and lost themselves in the shadows of the great woods, while their poor mother, with a scream of baffled rage and pain dropped crashing into the underbrush.

But the bear happened to be simply stunned by the shot, and so the farmer and his boys took stout ropes and tied her four feet together and slipping a stout pole between them, in this fashion they carried her down the mountain, and then chained her to a tree near the barn. For the farmer and his boys were very proud of their live bear, and proposed to exhibit their treasure to all the neighbors.

Oh, how miserable and unhappy the poor, little black bear mother was, tied fast to the tree, while boys and men poked at her and prodded her with sharp sticks, just for the sake of hearing her fierce, angry growls. Sometimes, when too hard pressed, she would even climb into the tree, to get away from her tormentors, but in vain; the chain was too short for her to get very far away from them all, so she just howled and howled.

"I shall have to put an end to that old bear; she's too noisy," remarked the farmer that night, as he went to bed.

The moon came up that night over Cushman Mountain, big and yellow, and afar off among the thick, dark spruces, even above the singing of the frogs, Mrs. Bear's little round, alert ears had caught the sound of an occasional, helpless whimpering cry, which seemed to her strangely familiar. It was the two motherless little cubs crying, hunting everywhere for their mother. Slowly but surely they were tracking her and even now they were coming down the mountain slope, and very soon the mother bear, straining her little red eyes, caught sight of the two little round shambling forms of the cubs, stealing from behind the barn.

The next thing they were all rubbing noses and "woof, woofing" together happily, while their mother fondled them eagerly, cuffing them playfully about with her free paw, almost forgetting about her smarting wounds, so delighted was she to have the cubs with her once more.

But time was flying fast; already had the old hoot owl come back from his night's wanderings, and gone to sleep in his hole in the sycamore tree. Pale yellow rays had begun to take the place of the moon which had set; dawn was on the way, and the bears realized that they must get away.

Fiercely tugging at the cruel chain Mrs. Bear began to worry it, giving mighty tugs and wrenches, while the two cubs whimpered a chorus of encouragement. Finally something gave way, and trailing a long length of chain behind her, old Mrs. Bear and the two cubs made straight across Balsam Swamp, and then scrambled and clawed their way up the side of Cushman Mountain, and not an instant too soon, for by this time the sun had come up, and day had dawned.

Then the little black bear and her cubs crawled into their den under Porcupine Ridge, and the tall, wild sweet ferns, the clematis and nettles fell over their door, and you never would have suspected that the bear family were safe at home again, and had no fears whatever for anything, for they had all gone fast asleep.

II

RING NECK, LEADER OF THE FLYING WEDGE

HIGH above the clouds, in the vast spaces of the heavens, the wedge-like flock of wild geese traveled. Unless your ear was very keen, you could barely catch the sound of their steady honking cry, far down below upon earthland, nor could you distinguish the faint outline of the wedge, unless there should happen to be a rift in the thick cloud curtain above which they flew.

All through the night they had journeyed, and for many long days and nights before, and the flock were becoming very wing weary; still, in spite of this, they never swerved from their course, and kept up their rhythmic, plaintive "honk, honk-honk, honk," as they flew. The call was necessary; it encouraged the weaklings of the flock, and kept the wedge together in unbroken line, for should one of the trailers fall far behind, he would quickly be swallowed up in the thick mists away up there in the trackless sky.

Alone, ahead of the flock, flew Ring Neck, the mighty old leader of the flying wedge. For years he had led the migrating flock; wide and strong were his great black wings, never swerving or faltering in their flight, while his loud, strident "honk, honk" sent back courage to the flock which trailed behind him. He it was who gave the first signal for migrating, telling them when it was time to leave the sheltered wildness of the southern lagoon, where they had wintered, with its deep coverts and long, trailing mosses, and start north.

Each year his kindred trustingly followed where he led them, thousands of long, weary miles. Usually the flock flew all night. If the moon chanced to be bright, you might see from earth the shadowy forms of the geese and flocks of migrating birds pass swiftly across the surface of the moon.

Just behind Ring Neck flew the next most important bird of the flock, Black Crest, a young gander who in time would probably fall into line as chosen leader of the flock, in case the old king should drop out. In fact, even now Ring Neck had often to fight for his high position, for each year Black Crest grew more and more jealous of the leadership, and but for the terrific beatings which the old leader gave him, from time to time, to teach him his place, the younger goose would certainly have been leader. But Ring Neck had no idea of giving way to this younger bird, no, not until his eyes grew too dim to pierce the mists, or his great wings too feeble to lead the flock.

"Honk, honk, honk," called Ring Neck steadily and clearly, slowing down his steady wing movement a trifle and floating. Then, at a signal, the whole flock began to drop very gently to earth, following their leader; down, down they fell. Now they were below the heavy white cloud masses, but still far above the morning mists. Ring Neck was leading them to feeding grounds and water. Finally, with swift wings he plunged straight through the mist curtain, and there right beneath the wedge gleamed a beautiful lake, spread out in the sunrise like a great silvery mirror. The flock were tired out, and glad enough that their leader had decided to rest. He seldom failed in his calculations, and could always locate water, no matter how high he might be flying, and always when he gave the signal to descend, they sighted the welcome pond.

"Honk, honk; come on, follow me," called Ring Neck reassuringly, plunging eagerly straight for the lake. Then, all of a sudden he slowed down, swerving a trifle, and uttering a warning cry to the flock to hold back.

Now what Ring Neck had seen with his sharp eyes was that, close among a thicket of reeds and cat-tails, he had sighted a strange flock of geese. Slowly fanning the air with his great wings, keeping himself afloat, and holding back the flock, Ring Neck swerved toward the strangers. There were six of them, all of equal size, and his keen old eyes flashed down upon them with curiosity and jealousy as he watched them floating calmly about upon the water. Never had he encountered such strange geese before; stiffly they floated, rocking gently upon the water, but the strange part of it all was, they neither dipped nor flirted their wings, or moved their rigid heads about as all his own wild kindred always did when they struck water. No, these strange geese simply held their heads in a stiff, fixed position. Were they swimming, resting, or feeding, or simply keeping still, biding their time, insolently waiting for Ring Neck to lead his weary flock to water, and then perhaps fall upon them, tired out as they were, and drive them afar?

Now Ring Neck was old and stubborn, and very brave, so he made up his mind not to give in to the strangers, but as he wanted the coveted lake for his own flock, he determined to drive them off.

Uttering a loud, strident scream of rage, he swooped like an arrow down toward the strangers; with wildly whirling wings he beat the air, trying to frighten them to rise from the water.

"Bang, bang, bang" snapped out the duck-hunter's gun, for he had been cleverly concealed, not very far away from his wooden decoy ducks, only Ring Neck had been so taken by the decoys that he had not seen him. As the gun spoke, down fluttered old Ring Neck the leader, and before the smoke and dropping feathers cleared, the gun pealed out and three of the flock fell into the water, and the hunter soon had them in his bag. But not so Ring Neck, for the shot had merely disabled one wing, so that he lay spread out, flapping helplessly upon the water, trying vainly to rise in air; no use, and soon with snapping beak, and strong, wild thrusts of his black feet he was fighting off the hunter, but it was no use; he was finally made a prisoner.

"Well, old fellow," commented the hunter to himself, "I've shortened your proud career for a while, I reckon; you're a mighty fine specimen of a goose; leader of the flock, I expect," and he examined, admiringly, Ring Neck's glossy head, and the changeable feathers of his neck, circled about with its silver ring, gradually trying to calm his wild struggles, as he smoothed his beautiful plumage.

Then the hunter made up his mind not to kill Ring Neck, for he had another, better plan. He resolved to train the wild goose as a decoy, and put him in among the wooden birds.

"Perhaps, who knows," remarked the hunter, "you will be able to call down the rest of your flock if they come back this way next fall. I'll try you and see."

So Ring Neck was spared, and then began his training as a decoy. Just so long as the wild geese continued to fly north, each morning, very early, Ring Neck was thrust into a bag and taken, with the hideous wooden decoys, to the lake. He soon learned to hate and despise the clumsy, imitation birds, and at first tried to rise and fly away from them, but his wing was not strong enough to sustain him, and so he always fell back weakly among them, where he would peck and jostle them about angrily; but as the wooden things never showed fight he soon tired of them and let them alone. Diving and feeding, floating naturally and contentedly upon the lake among the stupid decoys, he it was who heard the first faint "honk, honk" of a coming flock of geese; then he would become wildly excited and send back a loud answering cry, fluttering his wings and tolling the strange birds down to their doom. Not that Ring Neck wished the hunter to shoot them, which he always did if they came near enough. But somehow Ring Neck always hoped that the flock might be his own; perhaps he even hoped to warn them away. At any rate Ring Neck soon became a very valuable decoy to the hunter, who grew very fond of him.

As soon as the wild geese ceased to fly over, the hunter left the lake, for the season was over, nor would it open again until autumn, when the birds flew back south, stopping at the lake upon their journey to rest. So Ring Neck became a decoy no longer, but was allowed his freedom about the lodge. Strangely enough, he had lost all his wild desire to fly northward and join the flock, even though the association with the decoys had been galling. With each week his lame wing grew stronger, however, and finally his old, wild nature stirred within him, and he flew off alone.

Ring Neck became strangely lonely, for it was hard for the old leader to be without the companionship of the flock. After floating and feeding out on the lake all day, at night he would beat down the coarse grass with his strong webbed feet, and crouching low he would tuck his broad beak beneath his wing and try to sleep and forget his loneliness. But often he was disturbed, for a crafty fox or some enemy, a wild night prowler, would thrust aside the reeds, and then with whirring, frightened thrashings, and terrified squawks, Ring Neck would fly to the water for safety. At daybreak he would feed near the banks, plunging down deep into the mud and ooze at the bottom, searching among the snake-like lily roots and water weeds for fresh clams, crawfish and in the shallows for shoals of little silvery minnows.

One morning he rose to the surface of the water, flirting his great burnished wings, and sending showers of pattering drops over the lily pads, and suddenly stretching out his glittering neck he uttered a loud, hoarse call, full of pleading and loneliness—a cry of longing for his kindred. Then from a little hidden inlet, to his joy and surprise, came back a meek, answering reply—"honk, honk, honk."

With swift, steady strokes Ring Neck followed the call, and there he found her—a beautiful green-headed duck, one of his own flock. She had dropped out of the flying wedge, weeks before, and had not had courage to join them again; perhaps she had even been wounded by the hunter and had not been able to fly. At any rate she was very lonely, and soon Ring Neck made his presence known, and after consulting together, they built a beautiful nest, high and dry upon a little reedy island right in the middle of the lake, and there they raised ten young geese.

There were few lonely moments now for Ring Neck and his mate, for the young birds had to be taught to forage for food, and most important of all, as soon as their wing feathers grew, they must learn to fly, and strengthen their wings for long flights, for Ring Neck knew that before the lake filmed over with its first ice, the flock must be far away in the southern lagoon, where no frost or cold could reach them.

All summer long the old birds trained the young geese for their long journey, and then when the frost began to touch the tips of the tallest trees, down in the lowlands, and to nip the little fox grapes, the migrating instinct came to Ring Neck and his mate. Another bear came to Ring Neck; perhaps when the flocks began to move southward, the hunter would come back and once, as if to remind him, he heard the crack of the terrible rifle, off in the woods, and saw the thin trail of smoke, which he knew. That day he flew back almost panic-stricken to the island, and with his mate and family nestled hidden together in the thick tangles of water weeds all that night.

Early the next morning, before the mists had lifted from the bosom of the lake, they all took to the water to feed. But somehow, Ring Neck was overcome with his restless instinct of migrating, so that he failed to feed with the others. He would float about, nervously, ruffling his feathers, and flapping the water with his strong wings, uttering little short, wild calls to his mate, until at last she became as excited as he. Then, suddenly, afar off, from somewhere beyond the blue hills, Ring Neck detected a faint, strangely familiar sound.

"Honk, honk, honk-honk," it sounded, every instant coming plainly nearer and nearer, until Ring Neck, almost wild with expectation and excitement, would make little sudden flights above the water, screaming and darting back to his mate again and again. Plainly he was trying to urge her to join him in long flight. She flew with him a short distance, then back to the water, uttering little, reassuring quacks, then Ring Neck joined her, and they urged the little ones to follow them. All the time the great, wild flock were coming nearer and nearer, and soon they were hovering right over the lake.

Ring Neck rose from the water, giving a strange, unusual cry, then from far above floated back a ringing, answering challenge; he had been answered, and recognized. It was his old, lost flock, and at their head flew Black Crest, his enemy, their new leader.

Winging with great, wide, swift circles Ring Neck soon caught up with the wedge, then followed a whirling, flashing of wings, far up there in space; a handful of feathers floated down, and when Black Crest, whipped and beaten as he had never been before, dropped back into second place as usual, Ring Neck, their old proud leader, took his position again at the head of the flying wedge. Swerving low, almost to the bosom of the lake, he led the flock downward, calling all the time in loud, commanding voice for his family to join him. Back came the answering calls of his faithful mate, as she and the young geese rose from the water in a body, and took their places, falling into the tail-end of the wedge, as the great wild flock, headed by Ring Neck, went "honk, honking" away to the southern lagoon for the winter.

III

THE REVOLT OF TIMOTHY

A LITTLE gray mouse, who lived in the wainscot, poked its nose cautiously out of a crack beneath the hearth, intending to snatch a morsel of food from Timothy's plate, which always stood there, heaped with dainties, but the next instant the little mouse had changed its mind, for there sat Timothy himself right upon the hearth in front of the fire guarding his plate. So, with bright, bead-like eyes, trembling nose and whiskers, the mouse, taking courage, just stared at Timothy, monarch of the kitchen.

Such a majestic air had Timothy as he sat there in his own place, which none presumed to usurp; his silvery gray paws tucked neatly beneath his warm furry breast, his big, yellow eyes just mere slits of sleepiness. Timothy saw the gray mouse quite plainly, but he never felt hungry enough to bother much about chasing mice, and, just to show his supremacy, Timothy merely opened one eye and stared insolently at the mouse, uttering little muffled, rumbling growls deep down inside, which so terrified the foolish little mouse that he immediately scuttled off behind the wainscoting, squeaking as he ran.

After his nap Timothy lazily stretched first one gray velvet foot, then another, strolled indolently to his plate, turning over the food, carefully selecting choice bits, nosing out that which he scorned upon the clean hearth, for Timothy was a spoiled cat, and he allowed no one to interfere. Everybody waited upon him, moving their chairs even, for he was monarch of the hearth.

After his lunch, selfish Timothy took a stroll. Ah, if he only had suspected, everything would soon be changed for him in the kitchen, for even now the dearest little stray dog, with soft coat of white and tan spots, had been received into the family while Timothy was out. Upon his return he soon saw the little spotted dog occupying his place, and eating from his own tin plate.

Fiercely indignant at the sight, Timothy arched his gray back until the fur stood up in ridges, as he spat vindictively at the stranger, while his big yellow eyes glared with such sullen hate that the little spotted dog shook with fear. Still he did not offer to fight, or give back to Timothy his place on the hearth, and actually ate up everything upon the tin plate, while Timothy had to stand and look on, with deep, angry growls of jealous rage. Timothy felt sure if he stood there long enough he would be able to frighten away the dog, so he took up his position upon the opposite side of the hearth, and just glared and glared.

But the little dog was brave and did not go away, and soon Timothy decided to vent his displeasure upon the whole family by leaving the house altogether.

Of course they would be so anxious to get him back they would surely send the spotted dog away, and then he, Timothy, would return to the hearth. So Timothy went away. Vainly they searched for him, even setting out his tin plate each day filled with chicken bones to tempt him back. But Timothy resolved to punish them all, and the pampered fellow had actually taken to the woods, for his heart was so filled with bitter hate and jealousy that he simply would not return to the kitchen. Now the woods where Timothy wandered alone were wild and lonely, and in them were fierce "Bob Cats," ugly lynx with sharp, tufted ears, who snarled and fought at night, and many others whom Timothy had never met. The first night in the forest he crouched beneath a clump of spruces. Soon a hedgehog came grunting along, and when Timothy spat at the hedgehog it simply turned its back upon him. "My, you're a sad coward. I'll teach you a lesson," said Timothy; then he began to cuff at the hedgehog and worry him. The next thing Timothy did was to climb a tree as fast as he could, for the hedgehog had turned upon him and driven his nose full of sharp spines. Most of the night he spent miserably trying to free himself from the sharp hedgehog needles. Next morning he was hungry. In a certain tree he found a bird's nest, with three scrawny young birds, so he had just put forth a paw to select one for his breakfast, when down upon his back lighted the mother hawk, and drove Timothy off into the forest.

That night, faint with hunger, Timothy climbed a tall sycamore tree and tucking his paws beneath him tried to sleep. But he kept longing for the cozy, peaceful hearth which he had left, as chilly winds swept through the woods and moaned through the sycamore, making its brown, withered leaves flap and clatter in a lonely fashion, quite different to the customary cheery singing of the copper kettle upon the hearth. A family of hoot owls awoke in their nest in the sycamore. Soon they discovered poor Timothy, and began to peck at him viciously, hooting at him, and glaring at him with great, fierce eyes, so that Timothy hastily scratched his way down from the tree. Soon something soft and white came fluttering down from the sky, and little flakes of cold snow began to settle upon Timothy's gray coat, while the wind began to howl, and the storm to break. Where could he go? Poor, miserable Timothy! The snow lay white upon the ground, and Timothy took long flying leaps to escape it. Occasionally he would pause to lift and flirt his feet, for he hated to get them wet; besides, they ached with the cold. A thought struck him; he would go back to the house and see if the spotted dog was still there; so he crept to the kitchen window and peered in, and by the light of the fire he saw that his place was still occupied by the little dog. So off again crept miserable Timothy to the great cold lonely barn. He slept upon the hay, where the cold snow sifted down upon him, and the wind whined and howled over his head all night. For days Timothy stayed there; he managed to catch a few stray mice after a long chase, but soon his sides grew thin, his soft gray fur shabby and coarse and dark, while his eyes were furtive and sullen. But Timothy's proud, jealous spirit was nearly broken, and one night he decided to go back to the hearth. So he stole into the kitchen after everybody was asleep, and then a wonderful thing happened.

The little spotted dog stood up and welcomed him, wagging his tail so hard that his whole body shook, and he actually greeted poor Timothy with a bark of joy. Then lonely Timothy, pining for sympathy, ventured a trifle closer to the hearth, and the little dog sidled over to meet him, and actually began to lap Timothy's rough fur tenderly, whereupon Timothy, to show that he bore no further ill will, sidled and rubbed himself gently against the tan and white spotted coat of the gentle little dog. Then Timothy and his friend ate together from the tin plate, sat down upon the hearth, and Timothy began a whirring, buzzing song of contentment which might be heard even above the singing of the copper kettle, as he washed and scrubbed his neglected fur coat, making a complete and fresh toilet suitable for the kitchen.

The next morning when the farmer's wife came into the kitchen such a sight met her eyes; Timothy had come back, and slept upon the hearth nestled quite closely to the little spotted dog, and they remained fast friends forever after.

IV

THE LITTLE RED DOE OF DEER PASS

AS soon as winter really set in in the North country and the snow began to drift upon the mountains and deepen in the passes, the little Red Doe and her mate sought safe sanctuary with the herd, in the thick cover of Balsam Swamp, where the balsams and spruces grew dense, and there they herded together in their winter "yard," hidden away among the evergreen thickets where they fed all winter upon the mosses and lichens of the swamp. The herd would tread down the snow as it fell, and feed around the swamp in a circle, and when they had nibbled close all the moss and undergrowth, toward spring they would reach up and feed upon the tender budding shoots of soft maple and spruce and barks which grew overhead. While merciless blizzards raged all through the long winter, there they remained, for the deer always seek shelter in such a "yard," seldom venturing out, unless they are pressed by hunger, and the snow crusts are strong enough to bear their weight without breaking through, for the slender leg of a deer is easily snapped.

It had been a long, bitter winter for the herd in Balsam Swamp, and there were so many of them to feed there that by spring the food supply where they had foraged had become so scant that only the older, taller deer of the herd could reach high and pull down the tender saplings. Thus it happened, as is frequently the case through winter, that many of the young, tender deer died from sheer starvation, because they did not care to leave the "yard" and were not tall enough to reach high for food.

They were all very glad, at last, when the first signs of spring appeared, and the bluebirds arrived, and the wild geese, coming back from the southland, went trailing over, "honk, honking" through the mists, high over the mountains, in the early morning. Winter was broken at last, and the little Red Doe and her mate came out into the open forest. The mate, a fine young buck, with strong, pronged antlers, with which he fought many a battle for her, led the way, glad to be out in the freedom of the mountain passes once more, after their long retreat. Their sides and flanks were lean from long fasting and privation, but soon they were feeding upon the short, sprouting herbage of the valleys. The maples were in bud; food was plentiful enough now, and all the herd scattered, glad to be free.

All summer long the Red Doe and her mate ranged together, care-free, through the mountains, climbing high up to the summit of Mount Cushman, gazing across upon other mountain ridges, where the tall pointed spruces stood out like sentinels against the sky-line. Going down at night into the deep solitude of the valleys, where the deep, purple night shadows fall early, into the woodsy smell of balsam and spruce, which becomes doubly fragrant after dew-fall. Here are the deer passes, where they rest at night in safety.

They were never molested in their travels, and should a fox or lynx cross their trail, the mate would bravely charge upon it with his strong horns, and send it slinking away into the shadows. And so the pair became bolder and tamer, and upon moonlight nights they would come close to the farmer's dwelling; into the orchards to feed upon the early apples, and even find the gardens, where they did shocking work among the pea vines and young, tender, sweet corn. Almost every evening, just at twilight, you might see them steal forth from the spruce woods, cross the road together, and if they met a farmer, they would halt curiously to stare after him, heads held erect, gazing after him with great, gentle, inquisitive eyes, alert and wondering. Then, suddenly, like a flash, having satisfied their curiosity, they were off—over the stone fence together they bounded, and the next instant you caught just a fleeting glimpse of their short, white tails, held high, like a flag, vanishing, flashing in and out among the dark spruces.

They had one favorite resting place in Deer Pass, where the thick pines grew close together in a certain deep hollow, through which a brook bubbled musically. Here, deep down among the plumy, green ferns the Red Doe and her mate often stayed at night. Sometimes, in the early morning, if you chanced to pass that way, you might even catch a glimpse of two beautiful heads upon slender necks raised above the ferns, and if you did not come too close to their retreat, they would not offer to move.

Midsummer came, and then there were *three* deep hollows among the sweet-scented ferns in their retreat, and a little spotted fawn followed the pair. Beautiful was the little creature, with soft, reddish-brown coat mottled with white spots, which looked like snowflakes, and such great, appealing, innocent eyes. The Red Doe and her mate were so fond of the fawn that they never permitted it out of their sight. Those were very happy days now in the deer family. But a change was in store for them of which they knew nothing.

In the month of October comes the hunter's moon, and then the deer law is raised, up in that Northern country where the Red Doe lives; and the hunters are allowed to shoot the males for ten days, but must not molest or shoot the does or their fawns.

So when the maple leaves were red upon the sides of the mountains and the wild geese began to head for the south again, and the partridges to drum in the hedges, then came the hunters. The little Red Doe and her mate, and the fawn, had, by this time, become quite fearless of man, and almost tame, for nothing ever molested them; so, with no suspicion of their great danger, they camped in the old spot at night, for near at hand were sweet, frost-bitten apples, and besides, the fawn was not yet old enough to follow over long trails through stiff mountain climbs. So one morning they slept late in their old resting place, and the hoar-frost lay in little jeweled crystals, powdering their red coats as well as the ferns about them. Deep down, hidden together, they herded, and so they failed to see the hunter who came creeping stealthily toward their retreat, dodging warily from spruce to spruce. With gun in hand he stole, ever creeping nearer and nearer to their camping-place. Was it the cracking of a twig at last, or did the buck catch the man scent? Instantly he jumped to his feet, antlers held high and straight, waiting to give the signal of warning to his mate.

Too late. A loud report, a puff of smoke, and he fell, even as he gazed. In a second, the little Red Doe was off; off and away, the little dappled fawn following after as best it might. But alas, when the fawn reached a section of barb wire fence, it leaped too short, and fell back entangled in the wire. Meantime, the Red Doe, terrified and frantic, forgetting in her great panic even the fawn, bounded on and on, seeking safety in the deep forest.

When the hunter had secured his prize, the carcass of the buck deer, he began to follow the trail of the Red Doe, and soon stumbled upon the little helpless fawn. The little innocent thing knew no fear, and allowed the hunter to disentangle it from the wire. Then, thinking what a fine pet the little fawn would make for his children, the man carried the little creature home. After a time it became quite tame and used to the children, and so they built a small pen especially for it, close to the great barn.

Lonely and alone, after this, wandered the little Red Doe; all through fall she roamed, quite solitary, over mountains and through the passes, avoiding all the herd; she would mate with none of them. One moonlight night she strayed into the vicinity of a large barn seeking corn-stalks, and there, to her great joy, she discovered the lost fawn in its pen.

It was an easy matter, with her long, slim legs, for the doe to leap the fence, and soon the lonely mother doe was rubbing noses and fondly lapping the dappled coat of her lost baby. Again and again did the doe leap back and forth over the high board fence of the pen, vainly urging the fawn to follow her. But it was no use; the fence was far too high; the little fawn could not leap it, and so the mother doe had to go away.

But night after night the patient Red Doe came back into the pen with the fawn, bounding away with the first peep of day. Away, into the safety of the deep spruce woods, for she was no longer tame; she knew the terrifying fear of man, at last.

Soon winter shut down again, and the deep snow fell, and the visits of the little mother doe to her fawn became less and less frequent. And finally the fawn was taken into the warm barn, and she saw it no more. Then, the last time the doe failed to find her fawn, hungry and cold, in the midst of a great swirling snow-storm, she turned away, traveling wearily back over the old Deer Pass, over the trail to Balsam Swamp for shelter.

That year the herd was large in the swamp, where they circled round and round, feeding upon anything which offered itself as food, only trying to keep from starving until winter should break up again. By early spring everything within reach had been nibbled bare, as usual; then the stronger ones of the herd ventured out into the forests. The little Red Doe had lived through the winter, but she had fared badly, for she no longer had her mate to reach up, with his tall, antlered head, and pull down tender branches for her to nibble. She was very thin and weak as she dragged herself out of the "yard," aimlessly wandering, loitering, separated from the herd.

Night came on, and she heard the spring chorus of the "peepers," as they awoke, down in the bogs. Other night sounds came creeping through the great, silent places, and finally, close at hand, a sudden, wild, snarling yell echoed through the mountains. It was the cry of a hungry old lynx evidently out trailing game. The Red Doe was instantly alert. Was the lynx, an old enemy of the herd, trailing her? Then, before she knew where it came from, the lynx had sprung from an overhanging birch, and leaped upon her flank, burying its cruel teeth in her tender flesh.

A swift bound. The doe managed to shake off the clinging lynx, who was old and weak from lack of food. And before the lynx could gather itself together for another spring, she was off. Fleet as the wind she flew but she could never keep up the pace for long, for she had not the strength now; besides, the lynx had wounded her badly. But with wonderful courage she bounded on and on, leaping boulders and rough places, until she struck at last the old, familiar trail which led to the old camping place in Deer Pass. There she sank down at last, between the thick spruces, into a nest of brown, dried bracken and young fern shoots. Weak and spent she lay and rested the next day. By night she hoped to be strong enough to travel once more, for she must seek food.

Small and slim over Mount Cushman arose the crescent moon that night, and pale little stars twinkled overhead, but the Red Doe was too weak to journey on. Then, in and out of the shadows, among the pointed spruces, stole a slim, red figure on long, slender legs, its small head held erect, its soft eyes expectant and alert. And the Red Doe heard; she knew instinctively to whom those small, cleft hoofs, bounding so lightly to her over the mosses, belonged.

The Red Doe raised her slim neck with an effort, and peered over the tall brakes, and then out of the shadows, with little, eager bounds of joy, came her fawn. At last he had grown tall enough to leap the hateful pen, and all the subdued wildness of his nature had come back again with the return of spring, and guided by its instinct, the fawn had sought and found the old camp and his mother.

There they stayed together in their fern bed until morning, and comforted and rested, almost well of her wounds, the doe was able to travel once more. And so, just as the hermit thrush and bluebird started their morning chorus, the Red Doe and her fawn bounded off together, seeking new pastures in the secret places of the forest.

V

DAME WOODCHUCK AND THE RED MONSTER

DAME Woodchuck woke up early one Candlemas Day from her long, all winter's sleep. She stretched her cramped claws drowsily, then waddled to the entrance of her burrow, and scratched and poked away the dry leaves, with which she had banked up her door in the fall to keep out Jack Frost. Then, with the tip of her snout and round black ears outside the hole, she sniffed in a deep breath of the keen, frosty air. It was still cold, very, but the sun shone and the next minute she had cocked her head one side to listen, for she had heard a bluebird's note.

"Po-quer-ee, po-quer-ee. Spring is here; what cheer!" he piped.

Surely if the bluebirds had arrived, then the Dame must be stirring; but, unwilling to trust the actual announcement of spring entirely to the bluebird, she resolved to find out in her own way if spring had actually arrived. So out she crawled, and mounting the great flat stone over her home, she sat bolt upright, her little black feet held tight to her breast, then took a long, anxious look, first over one furry shoulder, then the other. The Dame looked for her shadow; if she failed to see it beside her, then she would know that spring had come, for always, in this way, do the woodchuck family predict the first arrival of spring. But if she should actually see her shadow over her shoulder, then she knew that the snow was bound to blow into her burrow just exactly as far as the sun's shadow shone in, and that there was going to be six weeks more of winter weather. And then, in spite of the bluebirds' call, she would have gone right back to sleep again.

But this time the Dame failed to see her shadow over her shoulder, which made her so happy that she gave a little sharp bark for sheer joy, and rushed inside the burrow to wake up the woodchuck Twins, and tell them the good news that spring had really come for good. Out came the Twins, yawning and stretching themselves, and when they were thoroughly awake, they all had a grand frolic.

Dame Woodchuck and the Twins had lived in their home in the middle of the clover field, beneath a great rock, for years. It was such a fine, safe spot for a woodchuck's burrow; you would never suspect where the door was. You wondered too how the Dame, who was very fat, ever managed to squeeze herself into such a narrow crack beneath the flat rock. But somehow she did, and like a flash, too, if she saw danger approaching. Beneath the great rock ran quite wonderful passageways, which led into many secret chambers; so the woodchuck family were never crowded for spare rooms, for year after year they had worked beneath the ground improving their home, digging with their little sharp claws and teeth. And best of all, where you never would expect it, was a secret passageway; down deep, then up over a stone, then to the right, then through a network of roots it led, and the first thing you knew you were right out-of-doors. This was the back door of the Dame's burrow.

And so if the farmer's yellow dog should take it into his head to stop off in the pasture and try to dig into the woodchuck's home, when he was quite busy digging at one door, why, they could all easily have escaped by the rear entrance.

Wild and beautiful was the country where Dame Woodchuck and her family lived. Clover, pink and sweet, covered the whole field, and not too far away the farmer had planted his beans. Beans and honey sweet clover the woodchucks cared for more than almost anything else in life. About sunset they would all crawl out, sitting up together, all three of them in a row, upon the flat rock at first, looking with contentment forth over the clover field; then, suddenly, perhaps the Dame would playfully cuff one of the Twins, and over he would roll into the deep clover, and then a regular frolic would begin, as they nibbled among the pink blossoms.

Close by in the edge of the woods a Hermit Thrush would often come at twilight, and sing his bedtime song, for the thrushes always sing themselves to sleep at night. And Dame Woodchuck, when she heard the first note of the thrush, would sit bolt upright, and listen critically while he sang his song, for it was very sweet and beautiful, and this is the way it went:

"Oh—holy, holy.
Oh—spheral, spheral.
Oh—clear up, clear up."

And each time the thrush sang his "Oh" he would sing it a bit higher, beginning first upon a low note. Then far off, hidden in the dark bushes upon the nest, the mother thrush would send back a long, deep "O-h."

This little song of praise which the thrush sang every night meant a great deal to Dame Woodchuck, for she knew when the thrush came to the edge of the clearing and sang, then there could be no dangers lurking about, because the Hermit Thrush is so shy he would never sing his lullaby so near the pasture when there chanced to be a spy at hand. So you see what a safe spot the Dame had selected, and also many others, who lived in the edge of the woods close by, the gray rabbit, and the chipmunks.

Now far across the clover field in the distance might be seen a long, dusty highway, which ran up over the hill, and from the top of the rock the Dame and Twins used to watch the farmer's teams as they crept slowly over the hill.

They were curious about them, but then they never left the road, so of course there could be nothing to fear from them.

But one day instead of the slow-going farmer's wagon, quite a different looking thing came tearing madly over the long road. The Dame and the Twins were almost paralyzed with fear when they saw it, and sat up straight and watched it with bulging eyes and chattering teeth. It had great yellow eyes, which blazed in the sun; its body was bright red, and when it came just opposite the clover field it gave a loud "honk, honk," and then the woodchuck family waited to see no more, but bolted straight for their door and inside, as quickly as possible, so that actually the Dame, in her mad haste, managed to scrape off quite a patch of deep brown fur from her back.

Very shortly after this, when the woodchuck family were taking a moonlight stroll to the bean field, the same monster came rushing madly over the road with its yellow eyes agleam, almost the size of the moon. At which awful sight the Dame and the Twins gave up their bean feast and tore home as fast as they could, going in by the back door.

In time, all the little wild dwellers of the forest near by came to know about the great red monster with its yellow eyes, its awful screech, and the odor of its fetid breath, which poisoned all the balsam, woodsy scents of the forest, and made them cough. What awful thing had come into their forest home and disturbed their quiet, peaceful homes? Even the Hermit Thrush no longer dared come to the edge of the clearing to sing her lullaby at twilight.

One morning, before the woodchuck family were astir, they heard a great commotion over their heads.

"Click, click, click, rattle, rattle," it sounded. And the Dame poked her nose out of the hole cautiously, and looked and stared in dismay at the sight before her scared eyes. A great red monster was being dragged over the clover field by the farmer's horses; the creature had sharp, cruel teeth, a long, shining row of them, and they bit and bit through the tall clover, so that it fell all over the field and lay flat. In a panic the Dame rushed to tell the Twins, and there they all stayed, deep down inside the burrow all day long, while the red monster rattled and bit its way through the clover over their heads. At night all was still, and the woodchucks, gaining courage, crawled forth into the field because they were very hungry. But what a sight met their gaze! The monster was no longer there, and the clover was no longer there; the field was quite bare.

So the Dame and the Twins held counsel that night, and stealing forth, they left their old home, and traveled far beneath the moon. Over swamps, and through unknown forests they went, until they finally reached a wild, lonely place beneath a mountain. Then they all set to work with a will and dug out a new burrow for themselves. To their joy they discovered that many of their neighbors had followed them, the gray rabbit, and the chipmunk family. And the very next evening as Dame Woodchuck came out to seek her supper, right overhead in a thick pine came the Hermit Thrush.

"O-h, holy, holy.
O-h, spheral, spheral.
O-h, clear up, clear up,"

sang the thrush joyfully, for he was no longer afraid; all the little wild things of the forest had sought safety, far away from monsters, in the deep wildness of the woods. And there the Dame and the Twins lived together happily for many years.

VI

TRACKED BY A CATAMOUNT

TOM and Fred Kinney were driving back from the little mountain village, where they had been sent from the lumber station, up in the "Slash" on Mount Horrid, to buy supplies for the camp. They took this trip every week, their father, overseer of the camp, trusting them to drive Ted and Tot, the mule team, down the mountain alone.

Mount Horrid, rightly named, is a wild spot, and the mountain roads leading up to the camp are steep and rough. One drives over this trail for about fourteen miles, then arrives at a plateau, and just above, on the ridge, are the lumbermen's shacks.

Darkness comes very early in these northern mountain regions, for the sun sets beyond the taller mountain crags at a little after four in the afternoon and it is twilight almost before one is aware of it. Suddenly the sides of the mountains take on a deeper purple hue, then in the dense forests of balsam and spruce the shadows grow black and blacker, and already night has come down in the valleys between the ridges.

The night bade fair to be very dark and early, but the boys were not afraid, for the two small mules knew the road well without guidance. They let the lines fall slack across their rough coats, while they munched sweet crackers, and talked together about the best places to set their new muskrat traps, which they had purchased in the village.

The mules crawled leisurely up the steep road, stopping, as they usually did, at a steep pitch to get breath, then plodding on again. All of a sudden, without warning, they began to act very strangely, rearing and plunging about in the strangest fashion, and snorting with fear.

"Say, they act funny, don't they? Wonder what scared 'em," remarked Tom, clutching the reins which had almost slipped from his grasp.

"Gee," replied Fred, "do you know it's gettin' awful dark; wish we were back in camp. We ought to have started back sooner, not stayed to see that ball game," he grumbled. For, to tell the truth, Fred Kinney was the more timid and cowardly of the two.

"Oh, don't be a fraid-cat, Fred. It wasn't anything much that scared the mules; perhaps a fox or even a porcupine crossed the road ahead of 'em, that's all," commented Tom, easily. "Look, it's going to be moonlight the rest of the way. Who's afraid? I ain't. Have another cracker."

The mules steadied down to their usual gait once more, and the boys shortly forgot their fears and were soon chatting away about their snares once again.

But if they had only known, and could have peered through a thick fringe of spruces, right on the very edge of a long, rocky ledge, just above the mountain road, crouched a great, tawny, supple, fur-clad cat; the very largest catamount, or, as it is sometimes called, the American panther, which had ever been seen in those parts. The catamount had started out to forage as soon as the first, long purple shadows began to climb the mountains. He was a magnificent specimen of the cat family, a male, and back in his dark den, which he had made beneath an almost inaccessible ledge of rocks, high up in the wildest part of the mountain, he had left a fierce, tawny mate and three kitten cubs.

The catamount was gaunt and half-starved looking, but he was also a good provider for his family, and when his mate stayed with the small cubs he carried her food; but his nature was so fierce and ugly that, whenever he chanced to bring home a supply of food to the den, he and his mate always had a fierce, snarling battle over the choicest morsels, and their savage howls and yells at such times were so fearful that all the other smaller wild things of the forest slunk back timidly into their homes, lest they encounter the dreaded catamount in one of his fits of rage.

Now, had there simply been one small boy on foot, or a deer, perhaps, walking up through that dusky mountain road, the catamount would in all probability, driven by his intense hunger and a desire to feed his young, surely sprung upon him. But somehow the sight of the sturdy little mule team and the two figures in the wagon disconcerted him, so that he merely stretched himself out over the ledge and peered curiously at them as they drove beneath him. It was this of course which had frightened the mules; they had caught the wild, strong scent of the catamount in passing.

The great tawny wildcat lashed its tail impatiently, and licked its lean chops hungrily, at the mere thought of what had escaped him; and then from sheer ill-temper and disappointment, because it had not been a deer, or something he could manage, he raised his angry, yellow eyes to the rising moon and gave a wild, blood-curdling yell of rage, a yell which cannot be described in mere words. It rose and rose, echoing through the dense forests of spruce, to be repeated back again from the other side of the dark mountain, ending in a horrid, whimpering wail, which reached the ears of the boys, and sent a chill to their very marrow; at the same time the mules broke into a wild, shambling canter, never stopping for steep pitches even, but keeping up the wild gait until they had reached the plateau, and finally the camp.

"Say, it was an awful yell. Didn't you folks hear it?" questioned the boys breathlessly, as they rushed pell-mell into camp, full of their story.

"And the mules were scared stiff, too, so they just put for camp on a dead run. Say, father, it must have been something pretty bad to yell like that and scare the mules so."

"Catamount," spoke up old Uncle Peter Kinney from the chimney corner, where he was patching a pair of moccasins. "Pair of 'em over Deer Pass way. Heard about 'em last week; guess they got hungry an' came over the Ridge after deer. Good thing you boys was in the team, I guess. Pesky varmints, catamounts; used to be pretty considerable plenty up North here when I was a boy; but lumberin' scared 'em off some, I guess. Good bounty on 'em, an' good money in a pelt, too, if it's right, son."

"Well, father, one thing; now there's catamounts round here, you've got to let me take the rifle into the woods when I want to," spoke Tom. "Why, if we only get the catamount, then I guess I could buy a rifle; couldn't I, Uncle Peter?"

"Guess ye could, son; but, first of all, sight your catamount," he chuckled.

Winter passed away, and gradually the boys forgot their sudden terror of the catamount, although farmers down in the valley reported that a pair of them had visited their barn-yards during winter and carried off sheep and even small calves, but had always got away; so plainly the catamounts were still lurking in the mountains.

One day Tom and Fred went off on the other side of the mountain to hunt for rabbits. The old yellow hound accompanied them, for although lame and decrepit, he was still keen after the scent of rabbits. A certain dense thicket of spruces on the edge of a plateau was the destination of the boys, because there the rabbits were always plentiful, the thick undergrowth forming a splendid cover. Although it was now early spring, snow still covered the ground, and the boys saw plenty of fresh fox and rabbit tracks. Tom shouldered the coveted rifle, proud in the assurance that he could handle it as expertly, almost, as his father. The boys examined the different tracks with keen interest, noting mink, deer, and the trail of other familiar wild things, for which they were always upon the lookout, being well up in wood lore.

"What's that track, Tom?" asked Fred, curiously, pointing to a light, skipping track in the snow.

"Deer. Say, can't you tell a deer's track, Fred? Oh, look! Somethin's been chasing that deer. See those deep, round holes right behind? The deer was running hard, too; he was being chased, all right, and knew it, too. Wonder what it was. I don't seem to know those deep, round tracks."

"Say, s'pose it was a bear, Tom?"

"Nope. Too far apart. Whatever it was, it wasn't shuffling along stirring up the snow in long tracks, like a bear does. It took great, long leaps. Look there," and Tom pointed to the strange tracks in the snow.

"Say, Tom, perhaps it was a catamount," announced Fred, suddenly.

"Why, I never thought about a catamount; perhaps it was," and then Tom clutched the gun a trifle closer at the mere thought of that awful, wild yell, which he had never forgotten.

It was growing late in the afternoon when the boys bagged their last brown cottontail rabbit, but Tom had scared up a covey of partridges, and eager to bag a few, the boys pressed back again, following the tracks of their old trail back through the spruces.

"Say, Fred, did you notice our old tracks back there in the spruces where we branched off?" asked Tom, suddenly. "Well, look here. Here they are again; and say, that thing, whatever it is, is following *us* now. See its tracks right here again. Say, Fred, we're being tracked, and I believe by a catamount," exclaimed Tom, excitedly.

"What'll we do now, Tom Kinney? Look, it's almost past sunset now," and Fred pointed with slightly shaky hand at the yellow glow of the sunset and the fast darkening mountainsides. Soon darkness would be down upon them, and they could not possibly go back over the Ridge and into camp before dark. Already they had tarried too long, and they knew it. For, as if scenting an approaching peril, the yellow hound suddenly lifted his muzzle and gave a long, dismal bay while his yellow hide arose in deep ridges upon his back.

"Tell you what let's do," suggested Tom. "We won't try for camp; we'll strike for Uncle Peter's old, abandoned shack. It's straight around the ledge here. We shan't be long reaching it; we can make it before dark. I guess we don't want to be out on the mountain to-night with a catamount or two loose, and chasing us. Why, he might jump down on us any minute from a ledge. Canada Joe said he saw one jump off a terrible steep ledge once and land on a deer's back, and he says they never miss anything they jump for, either."

Accordingly the boys made tracks for the shack as fast as they could travel. And sure enough, the catamount was not very far behind them, but was surely tracking them. Stealthily following their trail without showing itself, creeping warily in and out between the dark spruces, never losing its sight of them, the soft "pad, pad, pad" of its round feet muffled by the snow, its hateful yellow eyes gleaming and watchful, pausing when the boys halted, and loping on after them as soon as they started again.

The boys did not relish a whole night in Uncle Peter's old shack very much, but they knew that their folks would not worry about them greatly for frequently, when they were off hunting, they stopped off in some abandoned lumber camp, when they had gone too great a distance to reach the home camp. Ordinarily it would be a lark, but now they were slightly uncomfortable about encountering a catamount, perhaps a pair of them. But as soon as they reached the shack their spirits rose again, for the shelter of a roof, be it ever so humble, lends courage. To be sure the old shack lacked a door, for some one had long ago used it for firewood. The boys gathered quantities of pine brush, and soon had a great fire snapping up the rude stone chimney of the shack, which lighted it from top to bottom. They dressed and broiled their partridges, and ate their dry bread with hearty, healthy appetites, forgetting, for the time, all about catamounts.

But had they only known—straight out through the dense black cover of the spruce bush even now lurked and waited the great tawny cat, peering, peering, with its glowering eyes, right into the shack, simply biding its time, apparently, but growing every minute more desperately hungry and impatient to make an attack.

The boys tumbled into their balsam bunks and were almost asleep, while their fire dwindled and burned down low. Then suddenly the hound gave a little warning whine, and slunk back into the rear of the shack, his tail between his legs. Instantly the boys were wide awake, and just then came that fearful, blood-curdling cry, the yell of the catamount, and at the same time its dark, shadowy form bounded past the entrance of the shack, right outside the doorway. The catamount was now not a dozen paces off. It had tracked them to the old shanty.

"It's the catamount; I saw him. Look, look, Tom! There he goes again," whimpered Fred, suddenly stricken with terror.

"You keep still, Fred. Pile on brush on the fire, quick; that's what we got to do. It'll help scare him away. They're awful afraid of fire," and desperately the two boys worked, piling everything inflammable upon the dying fire until it blazed high again. Meantime the catamount, startled at first by the sudden glare, withdrew, but soon emboldened by its hunger back it came, ever nearer and nearer to the doorway; finally crouching just at the threshold, it made ready to spring.

With quick presence of mind Tom snatched up a great, glowing, resinous firebrand and hurled it with straight, sure aim at the catamount. It struck him squarely between the shoulders and scorched there, for he turned and bit savagely at the firebrand, snarling with pain.

All this time, between whiles, Tom had been fumbling with his gun and found, to his dismay, that he had but two shots left. He loaded, with desperate haste, not telling Fred of his lack of ammunition, but bidding him to keep firing the brands at the catamount.

"Now, Fred, I'm ready for him. You take a big firebrand in your hand, and then in case I miss him, let him have it straight between the eyes," directed Tom, and crouching low, with

THAT VERY INSTANT TOM FIRED

rifle ready, the boys waited for the catamount to come within range of the door.

Vicious with its burns and hunger, they had not long to wait for the appearance of the catamount; crawling, crouching low, cat-like it came, until it reached the door-sill of the shanty; then gathering itself, it made ready to spring into the room.

That very instant Tom fired. Straight between the gleaming, yellow eyes he aimed, and then, with a muffled howl of surprise and pain, the great, tawny beast leaped high in air, his bound broken; with a snuffling, snarling cry of pain he sank down, clawing and spitting. Tom had surely hit and wounded him.

"Look, look, Tom! See; he isn't dead yet. Quick, hurry and give him another shot. He's getting ready to jump again," shouted Fred. Sure enough, the catamount, now mad with pain from its shattered jaw, crouched for a fresh spring.

"Bang," went the rifle, Tom's last shot. And when the smoke cleared there lay the catamount, quite dead. Tom was thankful enough, as you can well imagine, for what would have happened if that last shot had not taken effect? For no boy can handle a catamount when it is fierce and desperate.

The two boys were far too excited to sleep again that night; besides, what if its mate should be hanging around somewhere! So they skinned the dead catamount, and the next morning, as soon as the first yellow rays of the rising sun touched the top of Mount Horrid, Fred loaded with the rabbits, and Tom with the rifle over one shoulder and the tawny hide of the catamount draped proudly over the other, tramped back over the Ridge to the home camp, displaying to admiring eyes the largest catamount pelt ever seen on the mountain.

VII

THE CALL OF THE MOOSE

THROUGHOUT the dense forests of the great Northland the call of the moose is heard late in April, when the herd leave their winter quarters or "yard" to strike forth with their families into the broader, more open country.

Monsall, the old King Moose of the spruce wood, had once more taken his proper place as leader of his own family. All through the month of March he had been quite content with his lot, and as timorous and helpless as any cow moose in the herd. This was simply because it was the season of shedding; his great branching horns were gone, and the newly sprouting ones were still in their "velvet" stage, so that they would have been of no possible service to Monsall in battle.

But now his horns were gradually hardening, and with the return of his shorn strength all the bold, domineering nature of the King had returned to him, and he was glad.

"Ugh-ugh-waugh, o-o," he called to his mate loudly and commandingly, and with his heavy antlers held proud and high he shambled triumphantly away. Blazing a wide, clear trail as he traveled through the thick bush, he led his timorous mate afar in the direction of new feeding grounds where beech and moose-wood bark were green and plentiful, and the forest pools full of water.

The call of the moose once heard, is seldom forgotten. It begins with a series of hoarse grunts or groans and winds up with a roar which booms and echoes through the most secret places of the forest, striking terror to the timid. Monsall, the King, was huge and ungainly. His great, powerful body would easily weigh over a thousand pounds, and his now towering antlers, when grown, would measure fully five or six feet from tip to tip. His coarse coat of brownish hair was now shabby, but he wore a fine, bristling mane of black hair, and a flowing beard of the same depended from his chin, which served to make his huge head appear twice its length. Fierce and bold was the King, keen in his likes and dislikes, but usually rather gentle with his mate in his fierce way, and he would do battle for her until he fell rather than own up beaten.

The pair went crashing onward, making their way toward the distant waterways and marshes. Long before you heard the crashing of the underbrush you knew, if you were experienced in wood-lore, that moose were on the trail, because the moose when it travels has a way of striking its hoofs together with a sharp, clicking sound like the striking of castanets, and the sharp sound heralds their coming. But for all the moose is himself noisy, he is perhaps the very keenest one in the forest to detect the approach of an intruder, for he readily takes alarm at the mere cracking of a twig.

Seeking a deep pool where lily-pads had already begun to spread upon the water, the pair took to the pool and plunged their great, velvety muzzles deep down into its muddy depths, dragging forth great mouthfuls of the water plants and their roots, and browsing contentedly together for hours. After the scant fare of the abandoned "yard" how good the luscious, succulent fare tasted to them.

Thus for weeks Monsall and his mate journeyed, until one day the cow moose deliberately deserted him, and hunt as he might, so cleverly had she concealed herself, he could not find her. She did not leave the hidden, mossy covert for days, for any length of time, and when she did, it was simply because, nearly wild from the stings of the black fly, which now swarmed in the woods, she sought water where she might stand to rid herself of her tormentors.

She hoped to find some near-by pool, but in vain; all the shallow, near at hand waterways were dried out, and she traveled long before she found a deep pool. She was very nervous and anxious to get back to the secret covert, for she had left behind her a baby moose. Wise was the cow to hide the little one from its fierce parent, Monsall. For so fiercely selfish or jealous does the male moose become, that sometimes for sheer ugliness he will trample out the life of a very young moose.

When the mother moose came to the pool at last, she gave a long grunt or sigh of relief and sank deep down beneath the grateful water, leaving just the tip of her muzzle and furry ears above the surface. The black flies, which had stung her until she was nearly mad, left her burning flesh and arose in a scum upon the water. So relieved and full of content was the mother moose that she almost forgot about the little furry fellow whom she had left back there in the secret covert. And so it chanced that a lumberman and his boy, who had been following a forest trail, came upon the covert and found the little moose. Lonely, and no doubt wanting its mother, it had stolen out into the forest upon its long awkward legs, and stood exactly on the trail when the man spied it.

Thus it happened that when the mother moose came shambling hastily back to her baby, uttering little rumbling calls deep down inside, just to let it know she was on the way back to it, she found the secret covert quite empty. For weeks she crashed wildly through the forest, calling it vainly; only her own lonely bellow echoed back to her straining ears, while afar off, in quite another direction, in the distant lumber camp the boy was learning to love the little moose, and had built it a rough shelter and yard not far from the lumbermen's shacks, lest it stray away, and he lose his pet.

In early autumn the mother finally gave up her fruitless search for the calf. Soon the herding time would be at hand, snows would fly, and then each family would seek the "yard" once more, and herd there through the winter. Overcome now with sudden loneliness—for already the hills were red with autumn tints; very soon after, up in the North Country, the first snow flies—the mother moose began to long for companionship, and so she began to haunt the old moose trails once more, and often send out her long-drawn, pleading call for her lost mate.

"Ugh-ugh-waugh, o-o-o" she bellowed, racing through the dark aisles of the tall spruces, whose far-away tops seemed to touch the blue sky.

One day, when she had almost given up her search, a loud, booming challenge, an answer to her call, came from a long distance away. Even then Monsall, the old King, was on his way to her and she was glad.

Now when the King Moose hears the pleading call of his lost mate, and makes up his mind that he will join her, should anything interfere with his plans, or hinder him in his travels to her, he is instantly on the war-path, and a most dangerous, terrifying foe for any one to meet. So when the old King Moose had raised his great antlered head, and after listening patiently, thought he had located the call of his mate, he was soon on his way to join her. Again came to him her welcoming call, oh, miles across the country, through forest and over mountain; but in spite of the long distance, Monsall had recognized her call, and he was coming.

Just as he had drawn in his breath to send out a mighty answering call, even before the echoes of his mate's cry had fairly died out from afar off, in quite another direction, came the unmistakable answer of a rival moose. Instantly the old King was angry and alert. What rival was trying to call his mate away from him? Whirling indignantly about in his tracks, his great antlers thrown well back upon his black, bristling mane, Monsall charged madly off in the direction of the rival call.

Time after time his mate wailed forth her call to him, and each time a reply came from the rival moose. The great lumbering hulk of the King tore wildly through the forest, felling saplings, and racing over giant tree trunks with no effort whatever, so wild with jealousy and full of rage was he, and at every new call of the strange moose his anger increased. His small eyes gleamed redly, and his heavy breath rushed like steam from an engine through his great distended nostrils, while his heavy jaws crashed together like the fall of a woodman's axe, as he ran blindly on.

Hours he ran; he would find and settle with this stranger who still sent his hateful bellow from afar, this rival who dared signal his own mate. His great antlers were now so terribly strong that he feared no other moose in the forest. Gradually he drew nearer the rival's hiding-place, or haunts; for the bellow was nearer and nearer. It was night when the King Moose reached the end of the trail, which led him into the lumber camps; but he had no fear of man now, so keen was he after revenge, and to lock antlers with his rival; only, somehow, that rival's bellow did not sound as loud or as challenging as his own. Surely his foe would be an easy one to rout.

The lumbermen had long ago gone to sleep in their shacks; they retire early, for their work begins at sunrise, and so the camp-fires smoldered, and it seemed like a deserted village, as Monsall halted right outside the slash or clearing, and stood stock-still to get his bearings, trying to gain sight of his rival. But no proud, antlered form rushed forth to do battle with Monsall. All was still; even the boy had been asleep for hours. He had given his pet moose its supper inside the yard, where he always fed it, had stroked and fondled its long furry ears, and the little moose had rubbed its clumsy, velvety muzzle affectionately over the boy's body, and allowed him to fit a rough sort of harness over its body; for the boy was planning to train the young moose to carry him upon its back. The creature had now become so tame that it readily followed the boy all about camp, and was a great pet.

So wrapped in sleep was the camp they paid no attention whatever to the strange noises and calls of the young moose through the night. In fact they had become quite accustomed to his rather queer attempts to bellow, so were not disturbed by the sound. For hours the young moose had been restless, sending out call after call from his yard, each call becoming more sustained and carrying wider as the young moose gained experience with his new gift.

So, while the fires burned low and red, into the camp came a great, shambling, hulking black figure; it left the fringe of protecting spruce bush somewhat warily; its great nostrils puffed across the smoldering fires, and sent the floating ashes whirling. Then it began to circle about the camp, drawing steadily nearer and nearer the moose pen.

"Ugh-ugh, waugh, oo," called the young moose, not very loudly or clearly, and as the sound came to Monsall he stood a second, then charged with raised antlers for the yard. Again the call, and this time the old King strained his great ears, perhaps catching a familiar note in the little moose call. Somehow it seemed to him not to be the loud, insolent bellow which he had followed and longed to do battle with its owner the moment he met. Then a strange thing occurred; instead of replying in his usual savage roar when he met an enemy, Monsall dropped his antlers gently and gave a gentle, unexpected low, which rumbled kindly, deep down inside his giant hulk, and meant only peace and reassurance to the little moose.

Then, through the darkness a great antlered head lifted itself over the high board enclosure where the young moose stood, timidly waiting he knew not what. Two velvety muzzles met over the barrier, the old King found and recognized one of his kindred; his own stray calf.

The lumbermen still slept on, and so they failed to hear the disturbance in camp and the crash which followed when the sharp, impatient hoofs of the King Moose tore down the board prison which separated him from his lost one, and gave it freedom—the freedom of the woods.

The old King and the little furry moose stood hesitatingly close to the dying camp-fires, Monsall to get his lost bearings, the little one waiting. Just then from far off came another long, pleading call, the mother moose calling again for her mate. Then the old moose lifted his antlers proudly, and a great and mighty challenge echoed through the camp and rang its way far over the pine trees to his mate. The great shambling figure of Monsall the moose took the trail once more, while close behind, right through the way which the old King blazed for him, followed the little one; they had heard and were following the call of the moose back into the forest.

VIII

THE LAST WOLF OF THE PACK

GRAY COAT, leader of the great Timber Wolf Pack, originally came from the wilds of Northern Canada, where the dense forests form safe shelter and cover for deer, bear, the red fox, and all the wild kindred who seek the silent places of the woods, far away from man. But one year lumbermen entered the forest with their whirring saws, and felling the tall pines, let in light into the dark places and uncovered their trails. The wolf pack was tracked and gradually thinned out and scattered, and Gray Coat, the big, brave leader of the pack, one day realized that he was just one solitary, lonely old wolf roaming the forests alone.

Gray Coat always seemed to lead a charmed sort of life, for no matter how skilfully traps were laid for him he never ventured into one of them, no matter how pressing his hunger might be. Often, nowadays, he would starve for days because he hated the whine of the lumbermen's saws, and they had frightened away the young deer, so that no longer did they come in early morning and at dew-fall to water at the old pool. Already ferns grew rank and untrodden over the old deer trails, and although Gray Coat watched and prowled about their old haunts, he never caught sight of even one red coat or flashing white tail.

At last the sides of Gray Coat began to show hollowly, gaunt and thin, and his coat became rough and shabby, a starved, baffled look gleamed in his sullen, green eyes, and his long, usually fleet legs were weak from fasting and often played him strange tricks; for sometimes when he chased a cottontail, because he had become reduced to such small fare, instead of the coveted tidbit, his lean, cruel jaws clicked together upon emptiness; he had somehow just missed the rabbit. Then Gray Coat instinctively knew that something strange and unusual had happened to him.

One night, too weak and lonely and disheartened to even start off trailing game, he sat solitary and unhappy just in the edge of a pine slash and lifting up his voice he howled and howled at the moon which looked coldly down upon his misery. It is during the winter that the wolves herd together, traveling in packs, but in spring they separate and mate. But although Gray Coat longed for companionship, there seemed to be no mate for him, for all his kindred had been hunted away from the old haunts. Had Gray Coat only been human, he would have wept bitterly; as he was only a wolf, he just sat all hunched up together, his lean snout low between his haunches, only lifting up his head to send his long howl through the woods.

Then somewhere, after a little silence, a very welcome sound came through the moonlit woods, the long, familiar cry of a wolf.

"Ah-h-o-o-o-oo, Ah-h-o-o-o-oo," it wailed through the long dusky corridors of the pines. And the next instant Gray Coat forgot all his troubles and, leaping to his feet, with all his strength he sent back a loud-quavering howl of command and pleading.

"Ah-h-o-o-o-oo!" To his joy, back came an answering cry, followed by a series of short, reassuring calls which sounded like sweetest music to poor, lonely Gray Coat. Each time the calls sounded a trifle nearer, and soon his sharp ears caught the swift sound of a "pat, pat, pat" upon the bedded pine-needles, and through the moonbeams came swiftly a welcome gray shadow. Gray Coat had found a mate. After they had nosed each other over, dog-fashion, and snarled together with snapping jaws, as is the wolf way of introduction, the two gray wolves, last of a great pack which had once roamed through the Canadian forests, trotted off together.

Silver Sides, the young wolf, was not starved looking or shabby of coat as her mate, and instinctively sensing his hunger, she led him to the remains of a deer carcass, and snarling together, they finished it. Then, with all his old, strong courage come back to him, Gray Coat took the lead, as he always had done, and together they ran on and on through the woods. For days and nights the pair traveled, just two fleet gray shadows, slipping through the silent places of the forest; skulking warily, they avoided the man scent, but always keeping together, for, by common consent, they were now making for a strange, new country and fresh hunting grounds.

But in one thing they had erred; instead of striking off farther north into the well-nigh impassable wild forests, where the lumbermen had not entered, and where they might have found plenty of game, and others of their kindred, they were traveling south, each day drawing nearer and nearer civilization, and, if they kept on, they would soon reach the Green Mountain country. Finally they came to the edge of a great swamp; its dense growth of dark balsams and spruces promised them a safe retreat, and surely, in such a wilderness, game would be plentiful once more, for not a trace of man could they detect. Little cottontail rabbits they saw in plenty, but, as time wore on, both the appetites of Gray Coat and his mate demanded wilder fare than mere rabbits. In vain they ranged together over the deer passes; the hunters had frightened away most of the wilder game. So, in desperation, the two wolves each day began to grow bolder and bolder, and even ventured down into the valleys beneath the mountains, forgetting their fear of man; soon they commenced to raid the farmers' sheep pens, and dragged away young calves to their retreat in the swamp. Then, as they were unmolested, they actually crossed the traveled highways at night, and often sent their long, wailing yells through the forests, until the villagers began to wonder what it all meant, because the wolf cry had not been heard in that section for years and years.

One farmer finally lost so many sheep he sat up nights to watch. And one moonlight night he saw the pair, Gray Coat and Silver Sides, come skulking like shadows from behind the granary. Quickly the farmer blazed away with his old flint-lock rifle, but he had not killed, only wounded one of the wolves and it got away, leaving a bloody trail of footprints behind.

Gray Coat had been hit and so badly lamed in one leg that he just managed to crawl back to the swamp before sunrise, and seeking shelter among the friendly spruces he lay there helplessly licking his wound.

As soon as the farmer realized that wolves were actually prowling around nights, he immediately set to work to trap them. But no trap could he find that would hold a wolf, so he invented a great drop trap, using the strong door of the granary for a fall. He then baited the trap with tempting fresh meat and waited for the wolves to come again.

Down in the swamp Gray Coat, sullen and ugly because of his lame leg, saw Silver Sides go off alone in the moonlight, night after night. He tried to follow her, for pangs of hunger were gnawing him, but his leg remained far too lame and stiff to travel upon, and so with a snarl of baffled rage he watched his mate slip off through the dark pines. Finally one night Gray Coat watched and waited impatiently for her to return. Would she find game, and perhaps bring him back a bone, as she sometimes did? At the mere thought his hunger seemed every instant to become more and more pressing, and the fever of his wound made him mad with thirst. Finally he dragged himself to a water hole, down in between the swamp tussocks, and lapped and lapped the green, scum-covered water. Then crawling wearily back to his retreat beneath a sheltering spruce, he waited and longed for Silver Sides to come back to him. All that night and the next day Gray Coat waited, but in vain; she did not return to him. Again the moon rose over the dark mountains, and filtered down into the swamp, and then, much to his relief, he tried his lame leg and found it stronger and better, so that he managed to spring out and catch an unsuspecting rabbit. Making a hasty meal, for he was so hungry he couldn't very well do anything else, he then struck off through the thick spruces, following eagerly the trail of his mate.

Once or twice, in his haste, he lost the scent, then he would run hither and thither with little baffled whines, his muzzle close to the ground as he made wide détours, circling ever wider and wider, round in a circle, until he struck the lost trail once more. It led him through devious ways down into the valley, straight to the farmer's sheep pen. Skulking warily in and out among the buildings, Gray Coat soon struck a keener scent, which led him straight to the trap. Strangely enough, the trap was not set, and as Gray Coat came creeping nearer and nearer, he found the heavy door dropped down. Baffled by this, he began to scratch frantically, digging and tearing around and beneath the trap with his sharp nails at the heavy door, for he certainly thought, by the strong scent, that Silver Sides must be back of the door. He gave little, whimpering, reassuring whines to her as he dug, just to let her know he was there, but received no reply from her. At last when his nails were nearly worn down to the quick, he stopped his furious digging. He was completely baffled; because, if she were back of the dropped door, she would surely have answered him. Then, suddenly, his miserable green eyes chanced to light upon a tuft of familiar looking gray fur; he sniffed at it eagerly. Yes, it surely belonged to his mate. Gray Coat tossed about this bit of fur, playing with it as a kitten does a feather, but he gained no response from the tuft of fur. Next instant he began to act like a crazy creature, racing madly in and out between the barns, for he had all at once caught a fresh, new clue. Following the new scent, it led him out behind a great red barn, and there it ended, for nailed against the barn door his despairing eyes saw and recognized the well-known but empty pelt of Silver Sides, his mate. Its plumy gray brush waved softly back and forth over the red barn door as if sending him greeting.

Gray Coat stood upon his long hind legs and tried to reach it with his snout. In vain; he received no welcoming snap from the empty jaws of the familiar pelt. Then, sitting down upon his lean haunches, Gray Coat lifted his head and sent such a long, wailing cry of despair and loneliness through the night that the farmer awoke and, grabbing his gun, started to hunt for the wolf.

But Gray Coat, having gained no response from the limp pelt upon the barn door, had left the barn-yard before the farmer got there.

Back on a great bare hill he sat, overlooking the now hateful valley, and trying to reason out in wolf fashion what it all meant. Soon, however, he had made up his mind—a time for action had come to Gray Coat; and lifting his head once more to the moon, he gave one last long cry, because of his lost mate. Then swiftly, like a gray shadow, he leaped away—for he had a long road to travel, because this time his instinct headed him in the right way, straight for the North Lands, where he would strike old familiar trails, fresh hunting grounds, and his kindred.

IX

HOW UNK-WUNK THE PORCUPINE MET HIS MATCH

IN the thick cover of the spruces, down in a natural hollow, where it was dark and still, and the fragrant boughs swept the ground, forming a perfect little bower, or tent, lived a very interesting family, Father and Mother Porcupine and their three young ones. So very young were the little porcupines, or hedgehogs, as they are sometimes called, that they resembled neither cubs nor kittens, but at first sight looked not unlike homely young crows before the pin-feather age; for when the little hedgehog is born, he is strange looking enough, his quilly armor being covered with a transparent skin; and besides, he is totally deaf and blind, and very helpless.

It did not take long, however, for quills to poke through the skin covering, and then sight came to the small, piggy eyes, and the little ones began to look more like porcupines. One fine day the wanderlust seized Father Porcupine, and off he strolled into the deep woods, and was never seen again. He had deliberately deserted his little family beneath the green tent, which is not at all an uncommon occurrence in hedgehog circles.

The little ones were quite often left alone now to shift for themselves, for their mother also took to wandering, and so one night when she had been gone all day, upon her return she found two of them missing. In the early twilight a stealthy, sinuous stranger had entered her home; just two little protesting squeaks came from beneath the hedgehog tent, and when the weasel left, only Unk-Wunk, the largest of the little ones, was left.

"Unk-Wunk, Unk-Wunk," grunted the lonely little hedgehog to his mother, as she peered in at him with her little dull eyes through the curtain of balsams, her cold manner showing no emotion whatever, for such is the nature of the hedgehog tribe that they rarely show much feeling over anything, no matter how tragic.

Now Unk-Wunk would never have escaped from the sharp teeth of the sly weasel had not his quills been longer and sharper than his unfortunate brothers. He had heard their terrified squeaks, and when the weasel made for him, he simply backed away, and for the first time in his life made use of his quill armor.

"Unk-Wunk, Unk-Wunk," he grunted fiercely, while the weasel glared at him savagely with its hateful, little red eyes. The weasel thought to himself, no doubt, what a silly, helpless thing you are to grunt at me so boldly. Who's afraid of your stupid "Unk-Wunk?" But the weasel soon found out his mistake, and backed out in haste from the hedgehog tent, his sly, pointed snout stuck full of cruel barbs, which it took him days to rub out, and taught him such a lesson that, ever after that, he never cared to cross the track of a hedgehog, and would frequently make a long détour whenever he chanced to spy one along the forest trails.

Unk-Wunk being of a particularly bold, independent nature, his mother soon left him, and went off to live with a colony of hedgehogs who had located their camp on a distant ledge. But somehow Unk-Wunk tarried in the old tent, for he loved the fragrant balsam scent, where overhead, when autumn came, the beech leaves turned golden yellow, and the brown nuts came rattling down in showers to his very door. Besides, just a short stroll away lay the marsh pools, threaded thick with succulent lily roots, considered, by the hedgehog tribe, the very daintiest eating to be had. All this lay close at hand, and as Unk-Wunk was naturally a lazy, indolent fellow, and did not care to hurry, or take unnecessarily long journeys, no wonder the place suited him.

Never, perhaps, had there been such an absolutely fearless hedgehog as young Unk-Wunk, because his first great success in driving off the sly old weasel had taught him the use of his quills, and made him unafraid of anything in the forest, whether it wore fur or feathers. He actually never bothered himself to get out of their very tracks, but would just stand looking very stupid indeed, and stare at them coldly with his little, dull eyes; if they presumed to come too near he would raise his armor and utter threatening grunts at them, so that usually they passed him by.

At twilight, when the old hoot owl, who nested above him in the beech tree, came out upon a limb and began to send out his weird call, and the hermit thrushes called to each other across the marsh-lands, then Unk-Wunk would lazily uncurl himself from an all day snooze, and leisurely stroll off through the silent places of the forest looking for a meal. When it began to grow frosty in the lowlands, and the nights were cooler, he covered longer distances in his raids, and even ventured into the lumber camps, gnawing his way through intervening boards of the shacks and sampling fat bacon, which he found so good that he would travel long distances to taste it. He stole eggs, too, and would manage one so deftly that he rarely spilled a drop of the golden contents, for he had a nice way of cracking a small place in the shell at the top, and inserting his tongue, or small paw, and never losing a morsel, leaving behind him just a pile of empty shells.

Strangely enough, the lumbermen's yellow hound, when he heard the steady "gnaw, gnaw, gnaw" of Unk-Wunk's sharp teeth through the shack flooring, would simply raise his head and utter little timorous, muffled whines under his breath, never offering to drive him away; if the truth were known the yellow dog was terribly afraid of Unk-Wunk. He would not hesitate to bay fiercely, chase a fox, coon, or even a bob cat, but once he had returned to camp with his jowls stuck full of Unk-Wunk's terrible quills, and after that he played the coward whenever he saw a hedgehog.

When you studied Unk-Wunk carefully, you might think him a very stupid, dull-looking animal. But back of his ugly, half-witted skull lay an alert brain, what there was of it. He dearly loved to play a joke, and for sheer sport would roll himself up into a ball and lie stupidly in one of the well-worn trails of the wood people; unsuspectingly, they would creep nearer and nearer the queer looking bundle. Then Unk-Wunk's dull eyes, peering out at them, perhaps, from beneath his hind leg, would sparkle with malice, and, like a flash, out would fly his tail, which held the very sharpest, most penetrating quills on his body. Then the curious one would usually go squeaking off on a jump, very much wiser than it had been before concerning the hedgehog family.

One autumn evening Unk-Wunk visited the marsh pool; his desire for a feast of lily roots, before the pool froze over, was keen upon him. To his dismay he found the pool already occupied by the blue heron family who were wading about upon their long, stilt-like legs for minnows or crawfish. Unk-Wunk realized well enough that he would be at the mercy of the herons' long, sword-like beaks once he entered the water, so he just stood behind the shelter of a spruce bush and thought out a plan to get rid of the herons, and have the pool to himself.

Waddling clumsily back into the deep woods, Unk-Wunk found a bed of dry beech leaves, and then deliberately laying himself down among them, he rolled his spiky body back and forth among them until every quill held a leaf; he was completely coated over with dry leaves, so that even his head was concealed. Then he crept warily back toward the pool and suddenly uttering a loud "Unk-Wunk, Unk-Wunk," he appeared right in plain view of the herons. Ordinarily the sight of a mere stupid hedgehog would never have stirred the wise herons, and they would simply have flown at him, flapping their great wings in his face, and sent him off. But as soon as they caught a glimpse of the strange appearing thing, all covered with leaves, and heard it actually cry out, with shrill, terrified screams they all spread their wings and flew off over the mountain, perfectly panic-stricken at the strange thing they had seen. It did not take the sly Unk-Wunk long to rid himself of the leaves, and plunge into the pool which he now had all to himself.

Now among the kindred of the wild Red-Brush, the Fox, is reckoned as the wisest of the wise. Still, in spite of his reputation for wisdom, he too had once been an easy mark for Unk-Wunk. In his travels Red-Brush was wont to seek his prey in all manner of curious places. He never failed to investigate hollow logs along the trail, for times without number he had run across an apparently vacant log, and discovered it to be occupied by a rabbit or some other easy prey.

Unk-Wunk had feasted well. A covey of partridges had strayed to his very door after beechnuts, and he had chanced to come home just in time to catch them. In vain did the brave little cock partridge drum at him, trying to mislead Unk-Wunk and turn his attention away from the mother partridge and her little brood, which scattered like fallen beech leaves in all directions. Unk-Wunk simply stood still and let the father Partridge bluster until he had become more emboldened by the seeming passivity of the hedgehog, which did not offer to molest him, and foolishly drew nearer, drumming in his very face, and so fell an easy prey to sly Unk-Wunk. After his feast all he desired was a safe, quiet spot to take a nap in. A hollow beech log lay conveniently at hand, and inside this Unk-Wunk crawled.

"Pat, pat, pat," came Red-Brush the crafty one, swinging jauntily over the trail, even before Unk-Wunk had a chance to close his eyes. They had sighted the fox, however, long before he arrived at the log, and instantly Unk-Wunk changed his position inside the log. Turning about he took care to leave the mere tip of his tail showing from the entrance. Then, with his little dull eyes twinkling, grunting softly to himself over the cruel joke he would play upon sly Red-Brush, Unk-Wunk waited for him.

Red-Brush advanced very cautiously. Ah, surely something had moved inside the entrance of the log. Soon the inquisitive yellow eyes were close to the opening. A sudden swift slap, and Unk-Wunk had played his joke. He grunted derisively as the fox tore off back to his burrow with a snout full of terrible quills.

Everybody knows that in an actual trial of wits the fox might really outwit a hedgehog. Humiliated enough was Red-Brush at the mean joke which Unk-Wunk had played upon him, and made up his mind, fox fashion, that he would one day get even with him. At last he took to dodging the trail of Unk-Wunk, hoping to catch him napping, for he had conceived a plan. The longed-for opportunity came at last. Chancing to stroll to the pool, the fox concealed himself in a leafy thicket to wait for game, which often came to the pool, and peering out from behind the rushes whom should he see but Unk-Wunk grubbing for lily roots. The sly fellow finished his feast, and so gorged himself with his favorite delicacy that instead of going home he settled himself at the top of a hill, just above the pool, for a nap.

The golden eyes of Red-Brush never left him; he bided his time until the hedgehog was fast asleep, then stole softly to the top of the hill. Unk-Wunk lay curled there in a round ball, and Red-Brush, with a swift blow of his paw, started the ball rolling swiftly down-hill. Unk-Wunk would uncurl himself before he reached water, for this they always do; with a bound Red-Brush reached the pool ahead of the ball, and just as Unk-Wunk gave a swift twist of his body to uncurl, the jaws of Red-Brush snapped together with a click, finding the unprotected throat of the hedgehog, and Unk-Wunk, the cruel joker, had at last met his match.

X

THE GHOST OF THE WAINSCOT

A LITTLE wire cage stood in a certain shop-window, and in it were two white mice, the funniest little fellows, with snow-white fur coats and pink, trembly noses, having long, silky, white whiskers, and eyes like tiny red jewels. All the school children had a way of stopping on their way to and from school to visit the white mice. They would stand close to the great glass window, pressing their noses quite flat against the pane, as they watched with delight the funny capers of the white mice, Fluff and Muff, for thus the children had named them. Fluff was the larger mouse, and he would spend hours whirling about in the small wire wheel, going so swiftly at times that all the children could make out was just a round ball of white fur revolving in space.

The wheel had a way of creak, creak, creaking merrily whenever Fluff whirled very fast, and, to tell the truth, this creaking was not wholly unmusical; and it had such a queer effect upon Muff, who apparently had an ear for music, that she would instantly commence a giddy sort of dance, all by herself, whirling madly around to the strange accompaniment of the creaking wheel just so long as Fluff kept up the music. All day long the two white mice frolicked together, only nestling down for short naps in their white cotton wool bed when they were quite exhausted. All this was entertaining to the children, who never wearied watching their antics. But one morning when they stopped at the great window, as usual, there was no wire cage with white mice in its customary place between the glasses of pickled limes and lollipops; in fact, the mice were gone.

So one boy, somewhat braver than the rest, volunteered to go into the shop and find out what had become of their favorites; indeed, if the truth were known, this boy had been saving up his pennies for a week in hopes that he might finally have enough to buy the white mice. Just as soon as he entered the shop he knew something dreadful had happened, even before he asked the shopkeeper, for right upon the counter lay the wire cage, broken and bent, its door gone, and the whirling wheel wrenched from its socket. The man told him that the cat had done it; had been shut into the store over night by mistake. So the boy, feeling very sad, just bought lollipops for his money, instead of saving up any longer for the mice, and went to school.

Now this is actually what *did* happen the night before, only the shopkeeper knew nothing about it, of course. When the great wooden shutters had been put up for the night, and all lights put out in the shop, it became very dark and still; to be sure the tortoise-shell cat had skulked between the shopkeeper's legs somehow, and slipped in slyly without his being aware of it. But, as it happened, she had not sneaked in for white mice; back of a certain barrel, over in the corner, she knew of a rat hole. That was what she had in mind all the time. She was not specially interested in white mice; she thought them freaks, at best.

So darker and darker grew the shop, and very silent, until finally a rasp, rasping sound came from behind the barrel. The cat crept stealthily across the floor on velvet-padded feet, and crouched expectantly. But the sly old rat did not come out just then; in fact he appeared to be moving something beneath the floor, dragging it noisily about. So the cat waited patiently; she meant to have the rat if she waited there all night.

"Pat, pat, pat," sounded a scurry of footsteps; it was the rat. He was getting ready to come out of his hole, and pussy gathered herself together for a quick leap. Boldly the old rat came forth, just as he had done night after night for weeks. A swift flash, and the cat had landed upon his back. "Squeak, squeak," shrilled the rat angrily, burying its sharp teeth in the cat's nose, and causing her to loose her hold a second. Then, before she could recover herself, the old brown rat was off and away. She covered his retreat toward the barrel, but the rat flew in another direction, up over the high counters, with pussy after him. In and out among the jars of pickled limes, lollipops and gum-drops he doubled, the cat following, always managing to head him off when he made for the barrel. Over among the goldfish globes into the shop-window he scratched his way, and finally tried to hide behind a great glass jar. No use; the cat's great, yellow eyes, blazing like automobile lamps, found him. Right over the cage of white mice leaped the rat in a perfect frenzy. Just then Fluff and Muff, almost frightened out of their wits at the dreadful commotion in their window, came out of their nest, and Fluff instantly began to whirl madly about in the creaking wheel, and pussy in her eagerness and haste mistook the moving wheel for the rat, and sprang with all her weight upon the wire cage, giving the old rat just the right chance to slip off to his retreat behind the barrel.

Topsy-turvy turned the wire cage; the wire door was wrenched off its hinges, and instead of the old brown rat which the cat expected to grab, she found herself with a little bit of a white mouse in her claws. What she did with Muff I am not quite certain; at any rate Fluff managed to escape, and off he tore across the shop floor, sliding in and out between boxes and barrels, half mad with fear, his little heart beating so when he paused that it shook his whole body. Finally he reached a green door; there was a little crack beneath the door, and Fluff decided to squeeze through. He came to a long dark passage next, then another door slightly ajar, and he entered the kitchen. The room was so large, silent and lonely that he was afraid; to his joy, he spied a little hole close beside the hearth and instantly slipped into it. To his surprise it was not so small as it had at first appeared to be, but it led in to a narrow, musty-smelling passage, which seemed to be very long, for he could not even see the end of it. The white mouse sat up on his little haunches, peering curiously about him, and even taking time to comb out his white silken whiskers, for strangely enough he felt very safe, somehow. The strange, musky odor was quite familiar to him; he sniffed at it with trembly pink nose. He recognized the trail of his kindred in that scent, and knew that the smooth runway had been worn by the travel of many pattering feet. Perhaps even Muff, his little mate, had passed over the trail.

Off scurried the white mouse at this delicious thought; he determined to follow the new trail to its very end. Suddenly a stranger, a little brown mouse, poked its head inquisitively out of a side track, took just one brief look at the white mouse, and instantly whisked out of sight. Fluff could hear her shrill squeaks of consternation and fear growing fainter and fainter as she hurried away. He stood stock-still waiting; perhaps she would return; but she never did. Instead, she went squeaking along the trail telling, in mouse language, no doubt, of the ghostly thing which she had met on her way to the kitchen larder.

This particular track, as it happened, was quite a favorite one and led for a long distance back of the wainscot. It had many turnings and secret passageways; even into the attic and down into the cellar it led. The rats often cantered over it at night with burdens of eggs or apples which they filched from the cellar; no wonder then the track was well-worn and smooth with the passing of so many pattering feet.

The white mouse, although he had never before seen a brown mouse, was anxious to make the acquaintance of the one he had met; perhaps she could show him the way to find Muff, whom he was beginning to miss terribly. So he boldly took the same road which the brown mouse had taken. He had not gone very far, however, before he heard a dragging sound ahead of him, and right in his path he saw a great gray rat dragging a large nubbin of corn. The white mouse stood stock-still, too frightened to run; he was so afraid of this monster. He trembled and shook so that his small teeth fairly chattered together. But he need not have been so very frightened, for the instant that old rat caught sight of the white thing crouching in its path it gave one long, terrified squeak, turning about in its tracks and scuttling madly off, even forgetting all about the corn nubbin in its haste to get away. Away from the ghost-like vision, the like of which it had never before encountered, in the wainscot passageway.

The white mouse gained courage at last, and being very hungry it ate the corn nubbin itself, daintily pulling off each grain of corn, and eating out just the heart of the kernel.

For days and weeks the white mouse roamed through the wainscot solitary and alone, shunned by every rat and mouse in the place, vainly traveling over the secret passageways, always hoping to turn some corner and meet Muff, his lost mate. How he longed for company, but he never could manage to get close enough to a brown mouse to become acquainted. One day he met a little company of very young mice; they halted and stared at him several seconds with their bright, bulging eyes. Fluff even ventured to give a pleading little squeak which meant to reassure them, but it was no use; evidently they too took him for a ghost, for like a flash they were off, and all he saw of them was five vanishing brown tails.

One day the white mouse chanced to discover quite a new runway which he hastened to explore. As he followed it the way seemed not quite so musky as the old trails, and soon he sniffed with delight a whiff of clear, outside air. The bright sunshine which met him as he poked his nose outside the hole almost blinded his little pink eyes, and the soft spring breeze ruffled his white fur coat, but Fluff enjoyed it. Peering warily about he leaped to a beam in the wood-shed, followed it until he had reached a knot-hole which led through the cow shed; from there he scuttled as fast as he could run, right into the old red barn, and diving deep into the hay he lay there hidden until he regained his courage and spent breath.

Now all through the fragrant hay run many secret passages, and as the white mouse entered one of them, ahead of him he saw a familiar figure; it was a mouse, and as she turned toward him, he caught a glimpse of white fur, and, strangely enough, the little mouse did not turn and flee away from him in terror, as the house mice had done. Fluff saw that she wore a coat of light brown fur, but that her breast was as white as his own fur coat, as were also her silken whiskers. At first he had thought it might be his lost mate, but as he came closer he saw that the stranger had large, bat-like ears, and bright, beady brown eyes; not pink ones, like his mate's.

Oh, it was pleasant not to be shunned, to be taken for a ghost. The lonely white mouse drew a trifle nearer to the mouse with the white fur vest, until at last they had actually touched noses, which, in mouse circles, means they had become fast friends. The stranger happened to be a little field-mouse who had wintered in the haymow, and had only come back to the barn in search of a few soft wisps of corn silk to begin her new nest with, for she had begun to think of building one out in the corn-field, just as she did every summer, so as to be close at hand when the milky sweet corn was ripening, because very small baby mice are fond of sweet corn in the milk.

And so, just because the little field-mouse was very lonely, she took pity upon the solitary white mouse and let him help build the new nest. They carried corn-husks together, then lined it deftly with the soft silk, and before the corn had ripened and turned yellow, there were five wee mice in the nest, and three of them wore brown fur coats, with white vests, exactly like their mother's, and the other two were pure white with pink eyes and noses. As for the cowardly rats and mice who still live behind the wainscot, and travel up and down its worn trails, day and night, they always peer ahead of them when they turn a sudden corner, exactly like a boy who is foolish enough to be afraid of the dark, because they always expect to meet the ghost which once haunted the wainscot, and drove them all nearly mad with fright.

XI

WHY THE WEASEL NEVER SLEEPS

IT is said by those who have a way of learning all the wood secrets and the intimate habits of the wild, that the owl always sleeps with both eyes wide open, the fox with but one eye closed, and that the sly old weasel, the very craftiest of all the wild kindred, never actually sleeps at all; hence we often hear the old saying, "You never can catch a weasel asleep." From far up in the North country comes the tale of how this actually comes about; why the weasel is never caught napping.

Once upon a time, oh, ages ago, of course, the weasel was not so full of craft, or so hateful and sly as he is in these days. Now he is about the worst dreaded of all the smaller creatures which wear either fur or feathers, shunned and hated by all his kindred, just because of his bad reputation. First, because of his cruel manner of dealing with his prey, for he just yearns to kill any young bird, or small stray animal which happens to cross his evil trail merely for the sake of the kill, and he does it so craftily that he will usually leave a mere pin-prick of a wound, perhaps, in his victim's neck to show just how it died. But always before he leaves he'll make sure to suck every drop of blood from its small body. That's the way of the weasel tribe; you cannot beat them for their cruel, crafty manners, and they'll trail their prey until it is completely exhausted, then fall upon it and kill it. The weasel always manages to save its own pelt, for in winter Nature changes its fur from brown to white, all excepting the tip of its tail, which remains dark. This aids the sly fellow to creep quite close to some unsuspecting little animal, because its white coat so blends with the snow its movements are not seen. There are weasels of many tribes; some of them are called pole cats. They belong to a race away back, when all weasels were sluggish, for in the old days weasels always slept soundly enough, just like all other animals.

And so it happened that away up north in the fur-bearing country, in a beautiful forest of giant spruces, which overhung a kind of a deer run, or trail, right between two ranges of wild mountain land, there lived altogether in peace and comfort a great many of the kindred of the wild. There the little black bear had her den and raised each year her little family, the brown hare thumped his signals against the great tree trunks unmolested and unafraid, the hedgehog grunted and grubbed in peace, and the red fox raised her cubs and they all gamboled together contentedly on a loamy side hill. Oh, they had great times there together, all living in harmony and unafraid, because they never encountered anything harmful in the forest, for man had not entered their spruce wood then.

On the edge of the mountain streams the gentle beavers came and raised their mud cabins, which the muskrat tribes came and studied and copied the best way they knew how, for 'tis a fact that long ago the beavers taught the muskrat all he knows about building his house. So there they lived beside the stream together; there were no snares set for them, no blue smoke ever lifted in clouds through the fragrant spruces, for there were no banging guns to frighten them. The only sounds you heard in the great forest in those days were made by innocent things: the gurgling of the little mountain brooks, the dropping of an acorn, the chatter of squirrels, or the crashing of bushes when the black bear and her cubs tore through the woods on her way to the pool to drink and wallow in the mud. Sometimes it was so still in the deep woods you could fairly hear the needles dropping down from ever so far above, down upon the mossy carpet where the deer herded. No doe or fawn had ever raised its head in alarm to see a rifle aimed between its gentle eyes those peaceful times.

First thing all the wild things knew, something strange had entered their peaceful forest. It began with arrows; the Indians were their first enemies. Gradually they learned to know about the strange whine of an arrow, and to fear the sight of a brown naked body, topped off by a crest of painted feathers. So some of them taking alarm wandered off into a wilder country, but most of them stayed behind, for you see they dearly loved their forest home.

Next thing that happened in the great North woods, the trappers arrived; they began snaring and trapping, and took away every little wild fur pelt they could get. Perhaps the beaver family fared the worst of all, because their fur coats would bring a fine price in market. But the greedy trappers did not stop at that; they soon got after the skunk family, the weasels, hares, anything which wore fur. They would cunningly set their snares close to a beaver village, and of course, in those days, the poor things were so trusting and innocent that they never suspected their danger; so of course they were not on the lookout, and all through the long winter they were trapped by hundreds.

By spring, which is the time when the beaver tribes get together and talk over their plans, because beavers usually increase so during winter, that in time some of them move out, and found other settlements, to make room, breaking up into colonies and each one going off. When the old king of the beavers called a council, he could hardly believe his eyes, for really there were so few of his tribe left that there were barely enough to found one good-sized settlement. About this time all the other little fur-bearing animals began to take stock; the skunks had been hunted out, and few remained; as for the weasel tribe, all that remained of a large colony was just the old king and queen of the tribe and one young kitten weasel.

Now this young one was as the very apple of their eyes, and had grown old enough to be cute and cunning, and company for the old ones; those days the weasels were about the happiest, most harmless family who lived in the great North woods. They slept then, same as all other animals do, taking plenty of long naps. One day when the old King and Queen Weasel were fast asleep, all rolled together in a fur ball, clear back in their burrow on the back of a ledge, just above the beaver village, a hunter happened to pass by their door, and the little weasel was out on the ledge frolicking, while the old weasels were fast asleep.

"Ping!" went a shot, and when the trapper went off he took with him a little brown fur weasel's coat hanging to his belt. Now the old weasels in their dreams had perhaps heard the echo of that shot; at least the old King Weasel imagined he had heard the young weasel's squeak of fear. So up he got in a mighty hurry and found the little one gone, and when they reached the edge of the ledge, there they found upon a bed of soft velvety green moss just the tiny, bare carcass of the little one, stripped of its fur coat.

Then the old King Weasel fell into such a horrible rage that it is said his very eyes turned as red as blood in his head, and that they have actually stayed that way ever since, because of his terrific anger. The result was that, being very wise, he and his mate conferred together, and they finally came to an agreement between themselves that it was all their fault; that if they had not been lazy and asleep the little one would never have met such a sad fate, so they resolved ever after that to be watchful and vigilant. They determined to live no longer a sluggish life, and said that no one should ever, ever catch them napping again, and they resolved to bring up all their tribe which should follow after them to keep to this resolution.

This was all very well, but 'tis said that they have never been able to overcome their terrific anger at losing so many of their tribe; this accounts perhaps for their mean dispositions, and makes them suspicious of everything which chances to cross their trails. His little red eyes, which he still retains, are sly, full of malicious revenge and hate; that's because he cannot help it, for the weasel was born thus. He has inherited his bitter spirit, and so he just kills and kills, just for sheer spite.

Now this movement and counsel together on the part of the whole weasel tribe finally set all the other wild things to thinking, for they all were victims of the weasel's enemies. So all those who had lost relatives through trappers or Indians held a mighty counsel together. In the end they came to the unanimous decision that they must drop forever their old, innocent trust of everything which chanced to enter the forest; that hereafter they must be very wise, always on guard against anything and everything which came near their trails, and more especially were they to be on the lookout for anything which resembled man.

So now you know why it is that the owl takes her rest with both yellow eyes wide open. This too is why, when the beavers are obliged to work in gangs all through the night, as they often do in time of flood, that they invariably select one of their number, a trustworthy sentinel, to guard their village. On some sightly spot the sentinel takes his stand like some brave soldier, always on guard, and the very instant he sees or hears anything at all suspicious upon the outskirts of the camp he immediately gives his signal of warning. "Slap" goes his flat tail against a log, and this serves to arouse the whole colony.

The eyes of the brown hare and her kindred were formerly gentle and unafraid. It is not so now, for they always wear a hunted, startled expression; actually at times they almost seem to bulge from their sockets with fear and anxiety. The hare is ever on the alert; she must never be caught unawares, and thus it is she always sleeps with her long, silken ears at just the right angle, so she can readily hear the snapping of even the smallest twig.

The muskrat and the woodchuck formerly built their huts with but one door; now they have two exits, and while the enemy is entering one door they are already off and away by way of the back door. They have learned their lesson. They are full of suspicion and craft.

As for old Brother Weasel, why, he is the very craftiest one of them all, and you can never actually catch him asleep any more, no matter how hard you may try to do so, and now you know why.

XII

MRS. WHITE-SPOT AND HER KITTENS

TIMMY lived in the red farmhouse at the foot of the mountain. Up the lonely mountain road, just above, runs a merry brook which crosses the road occasionally, and at such places it flows beneath a little plank bridge.

Over this road Timmy often traveled on his way to and from the cow pasture. It was a very quiet, lonely road, thickly hedged upon each side with bushes and overhanging white birches upon which Timmy loved to swing, and on the dark green spruces he found lumps of amber gum; so, altogether, he thought it a most attractive road. Just before the brook decides to cross the road, in one very secluded spot, it spreads itself out and makes quite a fine deep pool, which forms a splendid swimming hole. Not many of the boys knew about it, but all the little wild dwellers of fur and feathers, who lived near by in the forest, knew all about that pool, and often came there to drink and bathe.

One evening in late spring, before the maples were out, almost before the ice had gone from the brook, along came Mrs. White-Spot and her four kittens wandering down the trail. She crept warily around the bend of the brook, pushing her black snout cautiously through the dried ferns to make sure no hidden foe lay in ambush; then she marshaled her family behind her, uttering a series of reassuring squeaks, and they followed her down to the deep pool.

Mrs. White-Spot took up her position upon a large flat stone, just at the edge of the pool, and then went about teaching the little skunks how to take a bath. First she urged them all to venture out upon the flat stone, then, as one after another of the little skunk children followed her, she suddenly pushed each one of them with her snout off into the deep water of the pool.

At first they did not care for the wetting, and began to set up little protesting squeaks of terror, trying to scramble back again to the stone. But no sooner did they emerge from the water than, firmly, but gently, their mother pushed each one back into the pool again. Head over heels they went with a splash and a squeak. But finally when they had become quite accustomed to the water, they began to enjoy

MRS. WHITE-SPOT TEACHING THE LITTLE SKUNKS HOW TO TAKE A BATH

themselves, and splashed about like happy children, nosing and jostling each other in high glee.

Now Mrs. White-Spot was very proud of her little family, for they were as fine and handsome a litter of baby skunks as one might wish to see. They resembled their mother very much, and she was a beautiful creature, just about the size of the large family cat, with fur soft and fine, jet black, and so long that when the wind blew across her back it waved and undulated like a field of grain, with every motion of her body; and straight from the tip of her dainty, pointed nose, right across her back, ran a patch of pure, snow-white fur, ending at the tip of her tail, which looked precisely like a great soft black plume.

Mrs. White-Spot was so very much taken up giving her children a proper bath that she did not see that some one was eagerly watching her from behind a screen of alders. But there right on the edge of the plank bridge stood the farmer's boy; he had come padding down the mountain road with his bare feet, on his way from the sheep pasture, and his step had been so light the mother skunk had not heard him. The boy was very glad that the yellow dog had decided to stay behind and dig out the woodchuck hole up the road. At first, when the boy had heard the queer little squeaking cries of the skunk family, he thought it must be the call of a muskrat, swimming down stream, but just then he happened to catch a glimpse of flashing black and white forms in the water, and the boy instantly halted. Very fortunate for him that he did so, or Mrs. White-Spot would have spied him, and then his curiosity about the skunk family would have been satisfied for all time. The boy had not forgotten the occasion when his brother's clothes had had to be buried for a whole week once, just because he had unsuspectingly crossed the track of a prowling skunk, and now the boy, who had caught sight of Mrs. White-Spot and recognized her, almost held his breath and feared to move even a toe, lest she espy him.

Fortunately, the anxious little mother skunk kept right on bathing the babies, and at last, when she considered that they had been properly washed, she began to give little sharp, persuading squeaks, trying to call them to follow her out of the water. She left the flat stone and climbed out on the bank, and three of the little skunk children followed her, but the smallest one of all, evidently the "runt" of the litter, and a weakling, failed to follow the others, vainly clawing with his little black feet at the edge of the stone, and falling back each time he tried to climb out, uttering little helpless, protesting cries of terror.

Mrs. White-Spot halted, waiting patiently for the little one to climb out, but finally, when he failed to appear, she left the others and went back to the pool. Out onto the flat stone she scrambled, and then reaching into the water, she caught the little weakling by the nape of its neck, just as an old cat lifts its kittens, and placed him upon the flat stone. Just as she was turning away, the little skunk gave a sudden, helpless cry, and losing its footing upon the stone, over it went head first into the pool again. With infinite patience Mrs. White-Spot again turned back and went to his aid, lifting him out of the water once more, at the same time uttering little soft cries of encouragement; then she nosed the little one up the bank, urging him to follow after.

The boy had watched Mrs. White-Spot's performance with keen joy, not so much because he was greatly impressed by the charming little domestic scene which he had witnessed, as by the fact that he had been so lucky as to discover a whole family of skunks upon the farm, and because he meant to trap them, for skunk pelts are very valuable to a farmer boy. The boy was wishing and hoping to get money enough ahead to buy a certain "Flexible Flyer" he had in mind, and which he longed to own before the first snow came. If he could only sell five good skunk pelts, then he could buy his sled. So the boy made up his mind to track the skunk family and discover just where they made their home. Accordingly, he carefully climbed over a rail fence into the pasture where the brook ran, taking good care to keep out of sight and scent of Mrs. White-Spot, but meantime, hidden behind the bushes, he watched them at a safe distance. The little family were having the funniest frolic together, rolling over their mother and cuffing each other, like kittens at play, while old Mrs. White-Spot tried her best to seem dignified, but in spite of herself had to join in the fun occasionally, and would toss the little ones over with her snout.

Skunks dearly love to make their homes under some old building, and the boy felt almost certain that they were heading for an old sugar house further up the brook; so creeping stealthily along he traced them, and sure enough when they reached the old shanty, they all disappeared beneath its sunken floor. Before the boy went to bed that night, he had set five traps, baited in tempting fashion, close to the chicken house, and then with happy visions of the new Flexible Flyer dancing in his dreams he slept until morning. But when he went to inspect his traps, although he discovered that one of them had been sprung by some night prowler, not a skunk did he find, although several plump hens had disappeared.

The yellow dog bustled about importantly that day with his nose to the ground, uttering little baffled whines; evidently he had struck the trail of something, but he came back, finally, giving up the scent in half-hearted fashion, just as he usually did.

The following week, when the moon, big and yellow, came peeping out over Mansfield Mountain, down the little lonely mountain road, following the brook from the old sugar house, wandered Mrs. White-Spot and her small family, their piebald coats flashing in and out among the tall, dew-drenched grasses and ferns; the little ones following their mother closely giving squeaks of delight, for all skunks dearly love to be abroad upon moonlight nights.

Straight and sure, on went Mrs. White-Spot, and led her children right to the farmer's barn-yard, just about a mile below the bathing pool. Evidently she mistrusted that the boy had forgotten to shut up the hens that night, and that some of the foolish birds were roosting low outside the coops. In spite of much encouragement, the little weakling lagged behind the rest of her family; occasionally its mother waited for it to catch up with the others, when she would rub noses with him affectionately. But Mrs. White-Spot happened to feel very hungry, for as she drew near the farmyard she suddenly caught the game scent, and then she hurried on, eager for the great feast ahead.

Four foolish, sleepy hens, with muffled, terrified squawks, were quickly caught, and a stillness settled over the farmyard, broken only by the sound of little satisfied grunts; the chicken feast had begun. Then something happened, and a series of terrified squeaking cries came to Mrs. White-Spot's ears; it was the little weakling; he must be in danger. Instantly the mother skunk forgot her hunger and went to investigate. Sure enough, the little skunk was in trouble; he had accidentally got caught in one of the boy's traps, which had been temptingly baited with a chicken head. Fortunately he had been caught by just the end of one toe, and Mrs. White-Spot set about at once to free him. First she tried to pull the little one from the trap, then, finding she could not, she began with her little sharp teeth to try to gnaw the toe from the trap, trying to quiet the little skunk's cries of fear and pain by uttering comforting squeaks, and much nose rubbing.

It was just at this critical moment that the yellow dog, who had been fast asleep in the barn all the time, awoke and, suddenly becoming brave, scenting adventures, out in the moonlight, he bounded, overbold and ferocious, baying wildly, from the stable window, and in an instant had sighted the skunk family.

Then Mrs. White-Spot in great fear and sudden desperation gave a tug with her sharp teeth. The little weakling was free of the trap and the yellow dog, not knowing what was in store for him, bounded confidently right into the midst of the little family group. The next instant, to the great surprise of the dog, who had expected them all to run when they caught sight of him, Mrs. White-Spot turned and bravely faced her enemy. Poor foolish yellow hound, he knew nothing about skunks, and so he did not turn about and run. Why should he? What could such small black and white creatures ever do to bother him?

But the next instant the yellow dog found out his mistake, for with blinded eyes, smarting as though they had been filled with red pepper, staggering back in dismay, groveling and whining, and frantically trying to rub his head and yellow hide free of the sickening skunk scent which covered him he ran about in circles blindly digging up the earth wildly with his claws. All in vain; at last, in sheer desperation, fearing he knew not what, he managed to get away and crawl far out of sight beneath the barn. Mrs. White-Spot was revenged.

Calling her little family together, calmly they went back to their interrupted feast, and afterward lifting the little weakling in her teeth by its neck, and calling the rest to follow her, the skunk family all went back together over the moonlit road together, and finally reached the home nest and went to sleep, well content with their adventure.

Strangely enough the yellow dog can never be persuaded to follow the trail of a skunk; he will never forget his terrible experiences with Mrs. White-Spot and her family; furthermore, he had to be banished from society for days, and could barely be tolerated in the wood-shed, and so cowardly did the yellow dog become that even a sudden glimpse of the black and white cat and her kittens sends him bolting like a shot beneath the barn with whines and trembling body.

As for Mrs. White-Spot, she remained in her snug home beneath the sugar house for a long time, until all the little ones had grown up and were old enough to look after themselves, and the farmer's boy did not get the skunk pelts after all, but trapped muskrats instead, and in time sold enough to buy the longed-for Flexible Flyer.

XIII

IN THE BOBCAT'S DEN

THROUGH tangled jungles of wild blackberry vines and tall brake crept a tawny, mottled figure with stealthily velvet tread. At a distance the creature resembled a tiger, but following close behind its padding footsteps into the open, it appeared somewhat less formidable. Its head was round, but flattened at the top of its skull, and its jaws were beautifully marked and lined out with dark streakings. Its ears were fairly long and tufted, resembling in this respect its near relative, the dreaded Canadian lynx; its greenish, watchful eyes were alert and glittered savagely as it halted close to the edge of the swamp, where it was bound for its prey, but it had scented the presence of others, and had stopped to reconnoiter.

The solitary prowler was a full-grown, male bay lynx, commonly known in the northern country as the bob, or wildcat. This great cat resembles closely in its habits the tiger of the jungles, and loves best the dark, secret places of the forest; so, when the whine of the lumbermen's saws breaks the silence of the woods, the great tawny cat is ever seeking new dens, going back farther into the wilderness.

Already had the frost touched the maples in the low-lying grounds, and the forest trails were deep with fallen, yellow beech leaves, so that the comings and goings of all the wild things were rendered doubly silent.

In the heart of the swamp, for which the bobcat was headed, lay a sluggish pond, its waters black with rotting water weeds, and alive with catfish and pickerel. Close in the edge of the tall reeds lay an old flat-bottomed boat in which were two boys, who were fishing for catfish. Already, back in the dense forest surrounding the pond, it was growing black with coming night shadows, but the boys hadn't noticed it, because the fish were biting splendidly, as they always do just after sunset, leaping right out of the water with sudden splashes, in the center of the pond. Over the farther side of the pond a great night-bird was fishing, sailing low and screaming its uncanny cry as it dove after a fish. One of the boys suddenly noticed it, for the cry made him shiver.

"Say, Jud, what's that thing, anyhow?" he questioned.

"Just a loon, I guess," replied the older boy, easily, hooking a wriggling catfish, and taking it from his hook carefully, lest it stab his fingers with its sharp horn.

"Sounds awful kind of scary an' lonesome, I think, Jud, 'specially when it's most dark, like it is now. Say, Jud, let's quit and start for home."

"Well, we may as well, I guess," replied Jud, "but I hate to leave now; it's terrible good fishing. I got two dandy big fellows the last few bites. Guess we got enough, though, for a good mess, and we'll go before it gets any darker. Say, mother'll be awful glad of the fresh fish."

"Bet she will," replied Tom, as he carefully strung his catch on a willow withe. "Say, it's funny we can't get meat and things up here like we do home in Cleveland."

"Course, we couldn't expect to, but who cares? Mother's most well of her cough, staying up here," replied Jud.

"Say, Jud, I don't seem to remember this place," spoke Tom, as they plunged waist high through a forest of tall brakes into swampy, black mire. "Do you s'pose we're on the right road? Wish we had one of the camp men along."

"Oh, we're on the right track. If we keep straight on, I guess we're bound to strike that piece of corduroy road; then we're all right anyhow; that's the lumbermen's trail," replied Jud confidently. A long, weird, mocking cry came back to the boys from the direction of the black pond.

"There's that hateful old loon yelling again; wish we could shoot him," remarked Tom.

"Hugh, guess when you hit a loon, you'll have to be pretty old. Why, Indian Pete's lived all his life in the woods and in a canoe, and he's only shot one loon; they dive even before the bullet can reach 'em, and they can stay under water and come up a long ways off from the place where you first see 'em dive. They've got a crazy kind of a call; guess that's why they say some people are 'loony' when they go out of their minds. Say, Tom," suddenly exclaimed Jud, blankly, as he paused, "I—I don't see—— Say, did we come through all these dead woods?" Ahead of the boys towered a great forest of giant spruce, their dead bayoneted limbs showing gray and ghost-like in the darkness.

"Nope, we sure never saw 'em before. We couldn't ever get through 'em, anyhow, I guess," replied Tom.

"Well, I guess we're kind of off the track, somehow," agreed Jud. "We've got to go round these woods. I believe the corduroy road lies over that direction," and Jud pointed west.

Wearily the two boys tramped back over the trail, which was growing darker every instant, little suspecting that they were lost, hopelessly lost, in the jungle of the forest, and night was close upon them.

Back on the trail the bobcat kept padding silently on its way bound for the pond. It had come out into the clearing, and gave a muffled snarl of dismay when it had discovered the two boys. Back into the shelter of the tall reeds it crept, and lying there flat upon its tawny mottled stomach, it peered forth sullenly and somewhat curiously, watching the boys until they finally left the pond.

Then clawing and scratching its way up a giant spruce, it sent out a long, reassuring yell to its mate, for back in the bobcat's den, under a distant ledge, she waited with their three young kittens. From her lair she answered the call; it came back through the distance, echoing over the tops of the pines, and through the silent places. This was what the boys had heard and mistaken for the call of the loon.

On and on plodded the two boys, Jud leading the way for his smaller brother through the awful jungle as best he could, which was not very well, because every minute the way appeared to grow darker and wilder. At last, in spite of his hopeful words to Tom, Jud had to admit that they were lost, probably miles away from the home camp.

"What'll we do now, Jud Brown?" questioned Tom, almost in tears because of his blistered feet.

"Well, no use for us to go on, I guess, even if we could," replied his brother, rather dejectedly; "seems to be a ledge just ahead of us. We're climbing it now; guess we better find a dry spot and stay in it until daylight."

"Guess the folks'll worry some when we don't get back. Mother'll wonder why we don't come," said Tom, anxiously. "Why, look up there, Jud; there's a big, black mountain above, I should think."

"Yep, 'tis, and I guess it's old Hog Back by the outlines I can just make out," and Jud peered into the darkness, anxiously.

"Say, anyhow, it's an awful black, wild-looking spot right here; perhaps there might be bears, or panthers, or something, Jud," began Tom.

"Oh, well, there might be, but anyhow the best thing we can do is not to try to climb old Hog Back to-night. As soon as it's daylight I can find my bearings all right, for I know about where the mountain lies, but we'll camp under this ledge. Say, great luck, I've found two matches in my pocket. We'll build a fire and cook our fish. Why, we'll be all right 'til morning," announced Jud, his spirits rising. "There's a few hard crackers left, too. Oh, we're all right."

The ledge was flat and dry; a great bare stone formed its outer edge, but farther back it was overshadowed by a natural stone roof, and here it was carpeted by soft moss.

"Oh, look, Jud! See what I've found—a dandy little cave way back under here. It's full of dry leaves, too," announced Tom, joyfully. "Say, we can sleep in here; there's room enough for both of us."

"Sure," replied Jud, busy with his matches and some dry wood, which he soon had crackling and snapping, sending up a cheerful blaze which lighted up the dark, scary places and made things less creepy. Then he deftly skinned the fish, and raked a bed of coals, and they toasted the fish, which were delicious, even though they lacked salt. Then they gathered together quantities of dried spruce and built up a great fire far out on the flat stone at the edge of the ledge.

"Guess whoever sees our fire will think it's a beacon light, won't they, Jud?" remarked Tom, as he piled on dry wood.

"They sure will, Tom, and maybe some of the men from camp will be out in the woods and find us. Come on now. We'll crawl into our spare bedroom; we'll snug up tight and keep each other warm. There'll be a big frost tonight."

Soon the two tired out boys were fast asleep in each other's arms, while their camp-fire blazed high on the ledge, a regular beacon, as they said.

At least one curious one had followed its gleaming light, for with great, agile, anxious bounds, the bobcat, who had left its mate and kittens in the very den where Jud and Tom were now sleeping, was making its way back to the ledge. Growling and snarling because of the strange light, it crept nearer and nearer the den. The bobcat is by no means so dangerous a foe as the catamount or lynx, but when its young ones are in danger, it is fierce and dangerous enough.

The bobcat seldom climbed the ledge to its den, but would more often mount a tall tree, from where it readily leaped to the flat rock. The cat, having clawed itself up the tree, as usual, raised itself, clinging to a dead branch, and gave forth a long, terrific yell of baffled rage as it faced the camp-fire, which flamed up between it and its den, for when it had left the ledge for the swamp, back of that fire, safe in the den were the bobcat's family. It dare not leap over the glowing flames; still, unwilling to forsake its mate and kittens, it held its position upon the tree. Another fierce, more terrible yell, and the two boys came tumbling out of the den, and at the same instant the fire flamed up and they both saw the angry bobcat perched in the tree directly opposite them.

"Gee, what's that thing? A tiger, Jud?" gasped Tom, clutching his brother in sudden terror.

"Nope; maybe a catamount. Say, Jiminy, come to think of it, I guess we must have been asleep in its den," spoke Jud.

"What's to hinder his jumping over the fire and tackling us, Jud?" gasped Tom.

"Well, he won't, not so long as we can keep it built up high. Come on; hurry, Tom. Get more spruce, quick," and then both boys piled on more wood, and by the light they could still see the angry bobcat, who kept his position right opposite them, its green eyes glittering angrily, occasionally uttering its long, uncanny yell, which echoed back from the dark mountain and sounded like a dozen bobcats yelling in concert.

"Oh, just hear him yell; he'd jump straight on us, only for the fire. Say, we can't pick up much more wood round here," announced Jud, finally. "We can't climb up above either, on account of the rocky roof, and if we go down below he'll sure jump straight on us. What'll we do, I wonder?"

"Oh, say, Jud, what can we do, anyhow?" gasped Tom.

"We'll have to climb down an' risk his jumping, I guess. I'll go, Tom. I ain't afraid, much," spoke Jud, bravely.

Jud threw the last armful of dry spruce upon the fire, and was just about to climb down the ledge pluckily after more, when both boys heard a far-off, whimpering yell, which came through the woods from somewhere.

"Say, what's that, Jud? Another one of them things, do you think?" asked Tom, anxiously.

"Sounds mighty like one, but then it's a long ways off, down below somewhere."

"But if it comes up here, we can't fight two of 'em, can we, Jud?"

"No, but we can keep 'em off with clubs. Here, you take this one; it's got knots all over it; and I'll find one for myself. We'll crawl into the den and then if they chase us we'll whack 'em over the head," said Jud.

Just then another long, whimpering call came from down below the ledge, and then, instead of leaping, as it might, over the dying fire onto the ledge, as the boys had expected every instant the great cat would do, with its pointed ears laid back upon its flat skull the bobcat, from its perch upon the dead limb, sent back one long, answering yell into the night and began to slide and claw its way hastily down out of the tall tree without even deigning to notice the two boys. For, to tell the truth, the bobcat had only been interested in its little family all the while, and not in the boys at all, and so now with no thought but to follow its mate, whose appealing call had come to it from below, and anxious to get away as far as possible from the bewildering, hateful glare of the flames, which it hated, the wild creature soon caught the welcome, wild scent of the mother cat, and loped off into the dark silence of the night, leaving the two boys alone in safe, undisturbed possession of the bobcat's den.

XIV

WHY AHMUK THE BEAVER MOVED

THROUGH the summer days most of the wild dwellers of swamp and woods lead rather an idle, care-free life, as is their habit, thinking very little of autumn or winter, because it is a long way off; of course we have to except the squirrels, who are so very thrifty that they run back and forth, industriously storing their winter supplies all summer long. Then, too, there is the beaver family, who are perhaps the busiest creatures of all the wild kindred of the woods.

Wise and thrifty was Ahmuk, the King of a Beaver Colony who lived down in the swamp, and so old was he that actually tufts of snow-white hairs mingled with his stiff, bristling whiskers on either side of his round, furry face. He ruled over the company of beavers who made up his particular colony in the wisest manner, and kept them all busy, which is a trait of the beaver family. One often hears the remark that "he worked like a beaver," and you had only to watch Ahmuk and his family at work to understand just what this saying meant, for they worked away summer and winter, rain or shine, and, when necessary, all through the night, especially in freshet time.

One day, after Ahmuk had hastily called a council together, all the beavers, young and old, hurriedly began to tear down their old cabins beside the stream and move them higher up on the bank. The beaver cabins were built upon a solid foundation of sticks and brush, rounded off at the top, and neatly plastered over with mud, clay and sod, which they slapped into place with their flat, spade-like tails, which they use almost as well as another pair of hands.

The stream where Ahmuk and his colony lived ran through the heart of the great swamp, so they had many other neighbors; they never quarreled, however, for beavers are most amiable in disposition, and inclined to be friendly with all their wild kindred. Musquash, the muskrat, and his great tribe lived close by, and were a sort of cousin to the beaver family, for their habits were quite similar, and they also built their lodges along the banks of the stream. All through the rank grasses of the swamp, and threading the tall reeds you might see their winding, well-worn trails.

One day when Musquash the muskrat swam past the cabins of Ahmuk the beaver, he saw them at work moving their lodges, and paused to watch them, even forgetting to munch a prize of lily roots because of his great curiosity. He saw them all out upon the bank, working away for dear life, and hurrying madly, never stopping an instant, as they tore down all the old foundations and moved them far above the old site.

"Now I wonder what that's for?" thought Musquash to himself; "it seems to me that my cousins the beavers are always making themselves a lot of unnecessary work. Moving again? How foolish! Well, I don't intend to move my family again this season; the old huts are quite good enough;" and then Musquash, having satisfied his curiosity, lazily paddled himself down-stream leaving a long line of bubbles in the brown water to show where he had passed.

Now, if Musquash had but tarried long enough to ask Ahmuk why he was moving he might have been a great deal wiser, and thus saved himself much trouble and sorrow, for Ahmuk was so very wise that he knew that a big flood was coming very soon; and sure enough it did, and then the water rose and rose for days, until it washed away all the muskrat cabins, and even drowned out some of the little muskrats who were tucked away in distant chambers of the settlement, and were too young to swim and save themselves. But high and dry, far up on the bank above the great flood, stood the cabins of Ahmuk the beaver, quite safe; their work had not been in vain.

Soon after the great flood Ahmuk and the colony began to work building a wonderful, great dam, for they wished to make the stream into a pond. So they began to chop down great trees, gnawing them in such a manner that they cut the deepest place in the tree trunk next to the water, so that it would fall that way, and thus they would be saved the trouble of dragging the log a distance. Ahmuk and his tribe had such strong, chisel-like teeth that they could soon chop down quite a large tree, then they would gnaw out deep grooves all around the trunk, and chisel out the wood pulp in great chips, and just as soon as the tree got ready to fall, Ahmuk would slap a loud warning signal with his tail, and all the colony would scuttle away for safety to a high bank, when down came the tree with a mighty crash. When the danger was over and the tree down, back they would all come, and set to work trimming off the branches of the tree, precisely as the lumbermen do. They would then cut the trunk into suitable lengths for building the dam. It was great fun to watch Ahmuk directing the work of the dam building. Altogether they would push the log off into the water, then several of the young, strong beavers would shove it into place, and then they all set to work bringing gravel, mud and stones to fill up and cement the crevices together. They were always careful to build against the current, so that their work might not be washed away. Sometimes the large logs had to be drawn from some distance away from the dam; then Ahmuk would set them all to work, and they would actually dig out a channel right through the soft mud of the swamp, and float the log down to the dam.

At last the dam was finished and sentinels appointed to watch it day and night, for just as soon as a sentinel would discover a break in the dam he would awaken all the colony, and out they would tumble from the cabins, and work all night if necessary to make it safe and strong again. Sometimes Ahmuk even found it necessary to build a smaller dam below the large one to protect it. Then, too, when he found a low spot anywhere along the bank, he set them all to work building it up high enough to keep the water from running out of their pond. So you can readily understand that the dam required constant attention to keep it safe. When everything was in fine shape, the new pond soon became so deep that all sorts of strange new water plants, which the beavers loved, began to grow in the deeper water, while down from the smaller streams came trout, pickerel, and bull-pouts to live in the thick growths of water-weeds; and best of all, the pond lilies grew and floated upon the surface of the new pond, and every morning spread out their white, dewy petals in the early dawn; while below, in the dim, green depths of the water, trailed the long, succulent lily roots which Ahmuk and his family loved to feed upon.

The building of the great dam, and the making of the pond brought plenty of new neighbors to the spot: the great blue heron and her family, the kingfisher tribe, and many others, because the Beaver Colony had made the place so beautiful and inviting, and there were wonderful new things to be found in the pond. The long summer days came, and in the beaver cabins the family of Ahmuk was becoming so large that Ahmuk held counsel with the colony, and they finally decided that the time had come when the younger families must start out and look for a new place to live in. So, as the beaver family are very sociable, and always like to travel in companies, they all set off together one fine moonlight night to seek a new place for their dam-building, and to found another village.

The colony traveled together a long distance, for they really could not decide just where to settle, because each place which they came to seemed not just what they were looking for, not nearly as fine a location as the old village had been. Then, too, when the longing for wandering seizes the beavers they are prone to make long journeys into strange countries before they settle down. But finally Ahmuk, rather tired of wandering, and anxious to get back home, if the truth were known, advised them that they had found the proper spot at last, for he saw that there would be plenty of fine young timber close at hand for them to build a dam. So, altogether, they set to work and built a beautiful new dam, and then when it was finished Ahmuk, just to encourage the young beavers, and wishing to leave them comfortably settled, helped them build three fine roomy cabins on the edge of the stream; and making sure that they had plenty of tender young green saplings to nibble on in their larder, Ahmuk and his faithful old mate bade the younger colony farewell and journeyed back to their old home.

Now it so happened that the swamp had always been the safest kind of a home for the Beaver Colony, for seldom did anything ever disturb its wild inhabitants or enter the swamp. But slowly and surely men are beginning to search out and find the secret hiding-places of all little furry creatures of the wood, and while Ahmuk had been far off, at the very source of the stream up in the region of the tall pines, where the little mountain torrents and trout streams are born, a trapper had visited the camp of Ahmuk the beaver. He discovered the deserted cabins and the fine dam, and well knowing the habits of the beaver, he decided that they had simply gone off on a little pleasure excursion, for he did not believe they would willingly give up their fine dam and cabins, and thought they would return in time. So, very warily and cunningly, the trapper set his snares, because one must be exceedingly crafty and wise to trap a beaver.

Back from their long, tiresome wanderings came Ahmuk and his mate, and even though they were weary they both set to work making repairs upon the dam, for something had torn it apart; perhaps the hoofs of clumsy old Megalup, the caribou, or even Unk-Wunk the mischievous porcupine, who just loved to gnaw and gnaw, and destroy every log which came in his way.

When Ahmuk and his mate had finished repairing the dam, they went to their cabin to rest, but Ahmuk happened to remember a little chink which he thought should be strengthened, so turned back to the dam to stow away a few more stones, while his mate entered the cabin. Soon he heard her give a sharp cry of distress, and hurrying to the cabin he soon saw that she had been caught in a cruel trap, which had been deftly concealed beneath the cabin floor. Instantly Ahmuk set about trying to free his mate from the cruel steel teeth, which had nipped into her leg. Bravely they tugged and worked, trying to free her, but in vain. Then, in desperation, Ahmuk, wild with anxiety, with bulging, anxious eyes, set to work with his chisel-like teeth, and as gently as he could he sawed through the leg of his brave little mate, and she was free. True, she had to leave one little black foot behind in the trap, but she didn't mind that.

Ahmuk and his mate took to the water, and swam swiftly away, leaving behind them forever the beautiful dam and their comfortable cabins. And now afar off, in a spot which it is doubtful if any trapper will ever discover, live Ahmuk and his mate, with a fine new family. They have already built a new dam, and right in the center of it, watchful as ever, you may see Ahmuk himself sitting, erect as a soldier, a sentinel on guard duty; while close by among the thick jungle of the forest the whippoorwills and little brown screech owls keep him company, and his mate and the beaver children sleep safely, not so very far off, in their fine, new cabin on the bank of the pond.

XV

NICODEMUS, KING OF CROW COLONY

"CAW-R-R, caw-r-r, caw-r-r-r," called the leaders of Crow Colony, scolding and consulting together. It was spring down in Balsam Swamp, and they were preparing to disband and make their nests in which to raise their young.

On the very tip-top of a giant balsam, which had been broken off by the fierce winter gales, Nicodemus, king of the Crow Colony, had, year after year, built his nest. You see, the top of the balsam, being broken off, formed quite a broad platform, just the very spot for a crow's nest. From its lofty height the whole surrounding country lay spread out beneath like a great map. Besides, the high balsam was sure to be a safe spot, for the tree was very hard to climb, its branches growing at such a great distance from the ground.

Now all winter long the crows had lived together in a colony, but as soon as the sap began to ascend in the maple trees, and even before the thin ice was gone from the water-holes down in the swamp, they began to disband and to come forth from their sheltered retreats in the dense pine forests out into the open country.

Among the very first ones to commence housekeeping for the season was Nicodemus. He was the recognized leader, or king of the colony, because of his age and also because he was very wise and much the strongest crow in the flock. He always chose the most popular young crow in the colony for his mate, fighting and battling with the others for her company, and always getting the best of his rivals.

Now, secretly, Nicodemus was envied and hated by all the other crows, but not one of them had courage enough to approach very near the balsam tree, which Nicodemus appropriated for his home. He let it be understood quite plainly that they must leave him severely alone.

A fine, handsome fellow was Nicodemus. One would easily have selected him as ruler of the colony, for his great glossy black wings, when spread, were wider than those of any other crow in the flock; and his feathers glistened in the sun with burnished-bronze effects which made all the other crows seem quite dull and homely in comparison, and his round, sparkling brown eyes were so very keen and crafty that little escaped him. Nicodemus was also a great tyrant, and had never been whipped in battle—no, not even by the gray hawk who lived in the top of a giant sycamore, on the far side of the swamp. Occasionally the gray hawk would skim low over the nest of Nicodemus, but the old crow would simply take up a firm stand upon his home tree and send out short, insolent, barking crows after the gray, shadowy hawk, or boldly chase him back to the sycamore tree because, to tell the truth, Nicodemus feared nothing which wore fur or feathers in those days.

So when the maples put out their coral, pendent clusters of blossoms, and the willows and catkins down in the swamp burst forth, showing pale, tender green against the bare gray of the thickets, then in the loose, ill-made nest of Nicodemus, on the tip-top of the blasted balsam, there arose such a commotion and clatter that everybody in the Crow Colony was made aware that there were now four young crows in the family of the old king.

"Caw-r-r, caw-r-r," hoarsely and fretfully clamored the four scrawny young crows just as soon as they opened their filmy young eyes, waking up everybody about them for miles away with their peevish screams, even before the first yellow streak of sunshine broke over the swamp.

And once fully awake, these little pin-feathery crows almost distracted Nicodemus and his mate by their persistent cawing and fretting for food. Off would start both Nicodemus and his mate, searching frantically for food to fill the four ravenous mouths awaiting them back in the balsam tree nest.

Now all this hard work was quite a fresh experience to Nicodemus, king of the colony, for before he had a family he always foraged for himself alone, and whenever he chanced to pounce upon an especially dainty morsel of food he had always sought out some quiet spot, far away from his companions, where, quite unseen, he would proceed to hurriedly gobble down the choice bit quite selfishly. But everything was now sadly changed for, no matter how very hungry he himself might be in the morning, no sooner did he decide to eat his breakfast as usual than far away, from the direction of the giant balsam tree, borne to his ears by the wind, would come the fearful din of the four small, troublesome crows screaming for food. So, in spite of himself, Nicodemus, who was fond of his family in his own fashion, would go back to the nest with whatever he had selected for his own breakfast, and feed it to the young crows. Sometimes it seemed well-nigh impossible to satisfy their ever increasing appetites for, as they grew larger, they clamored louder and louder to be fed, and in spite of the combined efforts of himself and his mate they were sometimes at their very wit's end to find food, because, you see, other crows of the colony were also raising families, and food was not always to be found at once.

However, Nicodemus was so old and crafty that he soon learned to seek for food in odd places quite unknown to other crows.

Now in secluded spots the boys had set their muskrat traps, and in a certain spot by the brook where lived the mink family were snares and traps. Secretly Nicodemus visited them all, and, when possible, helped himself liberally to whatever he found in the traps. So that the boys never could understand why the traps were sprung sometimes, and occasionally a tuft of muskrat fur, or the tip of a toe left in the trap.

One day Nicodemus, after visiting all the traps along the waterways, found them all empty but one, and that contained nothing but a stale chicken's head, which Nicodemus saw lying quite carelessly upon one of the traps. He was about to turn from the unwholesome bait in disgust, for he craved something better, when, wafted on the spring air came the loud noise of fretful cawing.

"Caw-r-r, caw-r-r," squalled the young crows, which meant, "More, more, more."

At the unwelcome sound of their cawing, Nicodemus, fiercely hungry himself, and terribly desperate, made a quick grab at the bait in the trap, and the next instant he wished he had left it alone, for to his surprise and dismay some sudden force, unsuspected and unseen, clutched at, and bit into his leg, and he was held a prisoner. Oh, how he thrashed and beat his great wings, but the more he struggled and thrashed the tighter the steel teeth of the trap gripped and held him, until finally, just about dusk, the boy who owned the trap came and discovered Nicodemus caught in the trap.

"Nothing but an old crow caught in my trap," grumbled the boy in disgust, for he had hoped to find a mink. Then, just as he was about to throw out the crow, the thought came to him to take it home and tame it.

The next thing Nicodemus knew he was taken to the barn-yard by the boy, who drove a small stake into the ground and fastened him there securely. But Nicodemus thrashed about so madly that he soon broke the cord which secured him, and then the boy brought a great pair of scissors and clipped off the large wing feathers so he could not fly away; Nicodemus now became subdued and helpless. What a position for the king of Crow Colony. But worse yet was to come to him, for some one told the boy that if you will split the tongue of a crow it will soon learn to speak. Accordingly the tongue of Nicodemus was split, and soon, to the great delight of the boy, Nicodemus began to croak out something which sounded almost like "Hello."

Secretly, in spite of his humble appearance, Nicodemus was neither tamed nor subdued, and his heart was filled with hate and bitterness toward everybody; especially did he hate the forced companionship of all the tame barn-yard fowls,—most of all that of the great, haughty, strutting red rooster, monarch of the barn-yard, who never lost an opportunity of giving Nicodemus a vicious peck whenever he felt like it. And at feeding time, when Nicodemus ventured near the chickens to share a few kernels of yellow corn, once the haughty red rooster had fallen upon him and spurred him most cruelly with his sharp spurs, so that Nicodemus felt the effects of the thrashing for days and days.

Old Nicodemus was a very humble crow indeed these dark days. He lost all pride in grooming his former glossy, iridescent plumage, and became muddy and draggled. He would sit perched upon an old rain barrel in a corner of the barn-yard and croak and complain dismally to himself, hunching up his shoulders miserably, and uttering a peevish "Caw," and the new, strange croak which he had acquired, because of his split tongue, until finally he became so dull and uninteresting that the boy lost all interest in him and he was left wholly to himself; and thus it happened that his wings were left unclipped, so that all through the summer the wing feathers grew each day a trifle longer. Ah, Nicodemus' dull days were soon to be over, for one day, just about the time the first snow flurry fell, he spread forth his great wings and began to circle over the heads of the astonished fowls, cawing triumphantly and stridently; then, with exultant, happy heart, away he flew in the direction of Balsam Swamp.

When he reached his old nest it was empty. Nothing remained of it but a few loose sticks, and these were soon sprinkled over with snow. Oh, how lonely and unhappy was the home-coming of the king of Crow Colony.

Of course Nicodemus knew instinctively that his family had grown up and deserted the nest. Perhaps they had joined the colony for the winter, as was their custom, seeking some close retreat in the dense pines where they herd together for the winter months. He resolved to join the old colony. If he could only go back among his loved ones he would soon be welcomed again and take his rightful place as king of the flock.

All day long he flew heavily about over the swamps and mountains searching for the colony. At last the leaders appeared against the distant sky-line; they had flown over the mountain, and were coming back into the balsams for the night. Straggling and cawing they came, the long procession, and finally joining the last stragglers, Nicodemus flopped heavily along in the rear. And in the darkness of twilight he joined them, huddling close together in the dense green thickets. The flock had not recognized him and they gave him no welcome; evidently he was forgotten. But the next morning they discovered him in their midst, and just as soon as he gave forth his strange, new call they knew him only as a stranger, and one and all the whole colony fell upon him and, with fierce cawings and scoldings, drove him forth from their midst.

Poor, unhappy Nicodemus! Solitary and alone he flew off, deserted by the flock, and probably by his very own family as well. No one had recognized him. The winter which followed was long and cold. At break of day the deposed king would start off alone for food, and when night came, with heavy, tired wings, back he flew to the shelter of the pines in the swamp. There the winds howled and crooned above him, and fierce blizzards sent the snow swirling about his solitary retreat. It is hard for a crow to live alone, for with the colony, where there are sometimes hundreds of crows, they manage to keep warm by huddling closely together for warmth, and so do not freeze to death.

At last spring came, and Nicodemus, glad to be alive now, heard the old colony cawing loudly, and watched the great black band of crows as, greatly excited, they settled in a near-by sycamore to talk over and arrange the business of disbanding.

Then, unable to stand his loneliness longer, with swift, eager flight the old king of the colony joined the flock. In their excitement they did not heed him. But the eyes of the king were alert; nothing escaped them. Soon a young dandy of a crow, accompanied by his mate, spread forth his wings and headed for the stunted balsam tree, the old nesting place of Nicodemus. Then instantly all the old courage of the king came back to him, and with one mighty swoop of his great black wings, with loud, commanding caws, he followed the pair, caught up with them, and drove the presuming young crow away from the balsam. Nicodemus, king of the Crow Colony, thus resumed his place among his kindred as commander of the flock.

XVI

THE STORY OF RUSTY STARLING

RUSTY STARLING had a coat of glossy black feathers, all speckled over with rust colored dots, for all the world like a freckle-faced boy in summer time. His long, sharp beak was brilliant yellow, and he had such a funny, strutting kind of a walk which made him appear not unlike a dandy as he minced along over wide fields to feed. But Rusty's song was perhaps the queerest thing of all. It began, usually, with a few preliminary, creaking notes, which somehow reminded you of the noise made by a rusty swinging hinge; but occasionally he would change this note and burst forth into a beautiful, clear whistle, which he followed by a curious, throbbing call; and when he uttered this last call, it seemed to fairly shake his speckled body from the point of his yellow beak to the very tip of his long tail feathers.

Rusty was a foreigner; he sailed across the ocean to America in company with a little band of starlings, and was let loose in a large park. But one bright spring morning he suddenly began to feel strangely lonely, and longing for fresh adventure, he spread his wings, and off he flew to discover for himself a new country. At first he did not get acquainted with the strange American birds readily, for some of them chased him about, pecking at him viciously just because they failed to recognize him, for he was quite unlike any other American blackbird which they had ever met, and they were all suspiciously inclined, and unwilling to adopt a stranger into their midst.

But, taking it altogether, Rusty liked his new home exceedingly, and made himself quite at home in an old apple tree which chanced to be in blossom. The tree was simply riddled with knot-holes, and Rusty knew by experience that beneath the rough bark of the apple tree he could find plenty of fine grubs for the searching. The apple blossoms clustered thickly about him, all pink and white, and the air was sweet with perfume, while in and out, gathering pollen, the honey-bees droned and hummed in the sunshine. All this so charmed Rusty Starling that he began to pour out his strange rusty, creaking song as hard as ever he could pipe. Oh, what a fine spot the apple tree would make for a nest. Why, right below him in a knot-hole was the finest place he had ever run across. He felt very much overcome at the thought of building a nest in the apple tree, and the very idea caused him to change his first harsh, throaty notes into a wonderfully clear, beautiful warbling—the mating call.

Almost before his last note died out, Rusty's whistle was answered. First came the starling's creaking notes, then it merged into the same throbbing, inviting call as his own, and thus Rusty found his mate, for another starling had strayed away from the park flock.

Rusty never felt lonely after little Mrs. Rusty's arrival, and they soon made all plans for their nest building in the knot-hole of the old apple tree. It was such an ideal place, for the whole tree chanced to be hung about with many gossamer caterpillars' nests; there would be food a-plenty right at their very door.

During the mating days Rusty's coat of feathers underwent the strangest change, and you would hardly have recognized him, for he became very beautiful, having lost every one of his freckles. His feathers glittered and shone in the sunshine in colors of purple, green and golden hue, and he would flash like a jewel back and forth from morning until night carrying twigs and material for the nest in the apple tree.

The entrance to the nest was so very small that you simply wondered how a full grown starling could ever manage to get inside the door; but once he had squeezed inside, it was deep and roomy, and comfortably lined with down and hair. At sunset Rusty always took up his position on a twig close to the nest and gave a regular concert to his little mate, who sat away down inside the knot-hole brooding five young starlings. But really he or his mate had very little time for songs, for as soon as their pin-feathers commenced to sprout, the little starlings developed such fearful appetites that it took their parents every instant to find food enough to satisfy them.

One day when Rusty and his mate had gone off after food, leaving the little ones home alone, suddenly, as they were expecting the old birds to come home, a strange thing happened. Instead of food being thrust down into their wide, hungry mouths, a long, furry arm, striped with tigerish marks and filled with sharp, cruel claws, came creeping far down into the nest, and when it was withdrawn a baby starling went with it. Five times the dreadful tigerish arm was thrust down into the nest, and each time it took away a starling.

Rusty and his mate made a frightful fuss when they came back to the nest and found it empty; while there upon a flat limb sat a big tiger cat lapping his chops, and freeing his long whiskers from pin-feathers. They flew about his head, rasping shrilly, and trying to peck at him with their long yellow beaks, but the tiger cat simply blinked his eyes insolently at them. And somehow the starlings are of such a happy disposition that nothing ever worries them for long, and in a few days they were as happy as ever.

Autumn came, and soon the few apples left upon their home tree were touched by Jack Frost and became bitter, not very good eating; still Rusty and his mate loved to peck at them, for by this time food began to be scarce. Now, when October came, by rights Rusty and his mate should have gone south with all the other migrating birds, for at this time the starlings usually seek a warmer climate; but strangely enough, Rusty and his mate watched the bluebirds, the straggling flocks of geese and all their neighbors fly off, and still they tarried behind.

When cold weather came they left the apple tree nest, for the snow sifted down into it and blocked up their door completely. They flew off into the pine forests, and huddled closely together to keep warm. One day they were buffeted about in a great howling snow-storm, and Mrs. Rusty was blown against a barb-wire fence and her wing injured. Then Rusty knew he must find a comfortable spot for her or she would perish. So, urging her to follow him, he flew to a farmhouse, and there they perched upon a great chimney. My, what a beautiful warm spot they had discovered! The heat came up in great waves and penetrated their feathers, and best of all they could sit down inside upon a small ledge and be out of the storm.

Soon Mrs. Rusty's lame wing grew strong, and they were allowed to fly into the barn-yard and share the chickens' food. And upon sunshiny days they sat together upon the chimney and sang their rusty, creaking song together, for already beautiful visions of a new nest in the apple tree came to them. But one day Rusty flew off, and while he was away they built up a rousing fire in the old chimney to clear out its soot, so that when Rusty came back he could not find his little mate. She had been blinded and overcome by the uprushing smoke, and had perished.

He called and called, but vainly, and took up his lonely life again until spring time; and glad enough he was to welcome back all his old bird neighbors. He recognized them all in turn: the bluebirds, the flickers and the robins. And one great day as he sat lonesomely upon the old apple tree trying hard to keep cheerful by whistling to himself, suddenly he spied what at first sight appeared to be a black cloud floating right in his direction. The cloud moved rapidly, and finally began to come to earth. It was a great colony of birds, and somehow they appeared to Rusty strangely familiar. Soon a soft, creaking, crackling burst of song came to him, and instantly Rusty knew they were starlings.

Hundreds of them there were. They broke ranks finally, precisely like a company of trained soldiers, and settling all over the field, they began walking about with their little, quick, mincing steps.

Rusty gave one great, triumphant whistle of recognition and joy, and spreading his freckled wings he launched forth into the air and had soon joined the colony. And, wonderful to relate, much to his delight he discovered among the great flock another little starling so precisely like his lost mate that he was fully convinced that he had found her. And so when the leader of the great Starling Colony gave his loud whistle of command for the company to form ranks again, at his signal the whole flock arose, and making a wide wheel first, close to the earth, suddenly, as if they were one instead of a great company, they arose in the air and took flight, and Rusty Starling went with them.

XVII

WHERE THE PARTRIDGE DRUMS

ALL during the beautiful summer days the little Mother Partridge and her mate, the brave, ruffled cock, and their twelve brown chicks had lived just on the border of a deep wood, not too far back, so that when the little ones began to fly their flight should be easy. It was a fine, safe place for the little partridges, for they could easily run and hide from danger beneath the thick shadowy places of the pines, which towered so far above their lowly nest that only the soft, swishy whispering of their plumy tops could be heard down in the covert. The little ones grew rapidly, and were soon good-sized chicks; and they were very knowing, for the very instant their wise mother uttered her warning "cr-rr-r-r" cry, off they would flutter, looking, in their flight, for all the world like a drove of flying dead leaves; and strain your eyes as you might, after they had taken flight, you could never find where one little partridge had hidden itself. Instinct taught them to select a leaf or object which exactly matched their brown feathers, and then lie quite flat. There they would huddle until their mother gave a reassuring cluck, meaning "danger over," then out they would come in a little flock, and all this time while they lay hid, the little Father Partridge was never idle, I assure you, but took it upon himself, when danger came near the flock, to tell them just as far away as possible, and try to divert the attention of the enemy to himself in the funniest fashion. He would be so brave, even in the face of great danger, that he would boldly strut forth, all his feathers bristling, and the curious ruffle raised about his neck, and so bluster and strut and make such a ridiculous clamor that the intruder invariably forgot to see where the little chicks hid themselves. Then as soon as Mother Partridge and the chicks were off and away, a swift "whir-r-r," and before you knew it, Father Partridge had vanished as if the earth had swallowed him up.

The partridges always led their little chicks to the very best feeding grounds. Well they knew where the plump little red partridge berries grew thick in their deep green beds of moss, and also they remembered where in the deep mountain slashes the luscious red raspberries hung in ripe clusters; and sometimes they had to do battle with the screaming blue jays to drive them off, providing they reached the feeding grounds first. Brave as well as gallant was the little cock partridge. Off alone, on fleet wing would he fly upon private expeditions of his own, and when he succeeded in finding good feeding, he would mount upon a great log, or high place, and drum, drum, drum, beating his strong wings against his sides, and filling the forest with loud echoing calls—the call of the partridge for his mate, until she and the little partridges had followed him to the feeding place. Many a time when swift danger came upon them from above, and a cruel hawk swooped low after one of the chicks, then Father Partridge would raise his ruff fiercely and rushing forth, his barred wings and tail flaunted high, he would drum so loudly in the very face of the hawk that it would change its course and decide that it really did not care for a young partridge that day.

Gradually, as the young partridges became stronger and larger, they would venture forth into the woods upon short excursions on their own account, but they invariably came back to the home covert at night, where their mother would hover them beneath her soft brown wings, until they became too old, when they would all huddle together beneath the drooping limbs of a low falling spruce, or fly up into its lower limbs; for sometimes their instinct told them to sleep out of reach of Red-Brush, the fox, who sometimes strolled in the woods, near at hand, after dark. But somehow, in spite of the many warnings of wise little Mother Partridge, and fierce drummings of the father, one by one all but four of the partridge chicks mysteriously disappeared in one way or another, until when autumn came there were but six left of the large partridge family.

But they did not seem to mind that, which is the way in partridge families, and all through the autumn they had the very happiest times together that you possibly can imagine. The mornings were beginning to be keen and frosty, but their brown feather coats were thick and glossy, and they were so very plump from the abundance of good feed to be had, that they never minded the cold; it only made them wilder and livelier. Just as the first twinkling sunbeam filtered its way through the tent-like roof of their covert, then Father Partridge would take his head from beneath his wing; with a flash of his bright, beady eyes he would ruffle his crest, then "whir-r-r," swiftly his wings would take him off, skimming low over frosted ferns and brakes. Then five other "whir-r-s" would sound, and you knew that the partridge family were awake for the day, and had started off to hunt for their breakfast. Indeed in the partridge family it was meal time all day long in those autumn days, for they did nothing but feast continually, because that is the great festival time of the year for partridges. In the hedges the red choke cherries had turned black and hung in such heavy clusters that their branches trailed low, and the fruit was wild and juicy. The thorn apple trees, with their armor of bayonet-like spikes, were filled with scarlet apples, mellow and rich as a persimmon after the frost has ripened it, while over wayside saplings trailed long vines hung thick with little fox grapes doubly tasty because Jack Frost had nipped them. Then too there were beechnuts rattling down out of their yellowing leaves—all these good things to be had for the taking; no wonder the partridges grew each day a trifle more plump that autumn. Still, unlike the thrifty squirrel family, they were not wise enough to lay aside a hoard of food against hard, bitterly cold winter weather; they just flew about enjoying life.

So plump did the young ones become that at last you could not tell them from the old partridges. Then, all of a sudden, just as they were becoming recklessly tame and fearless, something terrifying and unknown came into the forest and drove every little thing which wore fur or feathers quite wild with fright.

"Bang, bang, bang," it sounded, the awful din, sometimes in the depths of the thick spruce bush, and again in the open, or down in the edge of the slashes; then up would curl an evil-smelling blue vapor, and one time when the terrified partridge family took flight two more of the young ones did not follow their leader to safe covert. Four of them, all that were now left, remained safely hidden in the depths of the deep forest for days, and at last the terrifying bangs were no longer heard, and they finally ventured out into the open once more.

By this time the maples, beeches, and the birch trees had all shed their dense leaves, and chilly winds, wintry and bleak, began to croon and whine through the dense coverts among the thick spruces. There the partridges sought shelter each night, and finally winter set in in good earnest and all the little wild creatures sought for warm, snug quarters. The squirrels huddled down in their cozy nests, all lined with leaves, and filled with a choice assortment of provisions, and old Dame Woodchuck had long ago crept into her burrow, deep down in the brown earth, and closed up her door for the winter; not until Candlemas Day would she venture to even stick her nose out-of-doors again. Still, there were plenty who did not care to idle and sleep all through the cold weather, so there was still plenty of life left in the forest.

After the first deep snow the partridges remained hidden in some deep, warm covert among the thick, sheltering pines, coming forth into the open only when they wished to feed upon chance dried berries which the snow and winds had left clinging to bare branches; but for the most part all the birds which had not gone south kept to the deep woods for shelter.

Now right in the heart of a balsam pine lived a great snowy owl, which had drifted from its kindred down from the far North, and taken up its solitary home close to the partridge covert. The great, wise owl thought herself perfectly safe, no doubt, in such a lofty home; so, a few months before, she had laid two beautiful snowy eggs in her retreat, which in time became two small owlets, with such comical, fuzzy, round faces, and large yellow eyes. The great snowy mother owl loved them as only a mother owl knows how, almost wearing herself out to hunt food for them, both day and night. One day when the great snowy owl came back to the balsam pine she arrived just in time to see a sinuous, brown, fur-coated stranger hastily claw himself down from her nest, and dashing swiftly and angrily at him, she managed to clutch just a tuft of his brown fur. He had slipped away, and her nest was empty;

and all night long, far above the spot where the partridges nested, the great snowy owl cried out: "Who-who-wo-wo-wo-o-o," and from that day she nested alone and began to watch and watch for the reappearance of that hateful, sinuous, brown-coated stranger who had stolen the young owl babies, but she watched in vain.

Fiercely raged the great northern blizzards and sometimes when the partridges ventured forth from their coverts when hard pressed with hunger the heavy winds would seize them and dash them roughly about, so that spent and weary they were often forced to come back to shelter without tasting food for hours. Still, in certain places known to the partridges there were still pine cones a-plenty, and in between the brown husk-like layers of the cones they found little nutty seeds of the pine, while beneath, in sheltered spots which the snow did not cover, they scratched for partridge berries, wintergreen plums, and an occasional beechnut which the squirrels had not found. Searching and keen were the wintry winds, which sometimes stung through their feather coats, so they would huddle close together beneath the shelter of a great log, or where pine branches swept low. One day a great storm raged which lasted for many days, and the giant pines rocked so mightily that none of the wild creatures ventured out as long as it lasted. The partridges huddled closely together upon the ground for warmth, and gradually the snow sifted and filtered its way through the forest until it had finally covered everything, even the partridges, who looked like little mounds of snow. Strangely enough they were warm and comfortable beneath their snow coverlet, for the snow arched over each sleek, brown back, forming a little shelter or hut over them, not unlike those small snow huts which the Laps build; and if you could have peeped beneath, you might have seen four pairs of very bright, alert eyes peeping from a tiny opening in their snow covering; that is, when the partridges were not fast asleep.

When the snowflakes began to come down slower and slower, and almost cease, then many of the wild things began to grow very hungry and ventured forth. A sly old weasel started out first, and soon his lithe, snake-like body was skimming silently through the pathless, silent forest, leaving queer little tracks in the soft snow as he traveled. Once in the deep pines he began to peer about for prey; in and out among the brown underbrush he crept, being careful that no twig should snap beneath him to betray his coming. Nothing seemed to be stirring yet; plainly everything was still asleep. But far up above in the giant pine above him the weasel failed to notice that a certain knot-hole was completely filled by a great, round, snowy face lighted by glittering, angry eyes, of pale yellow. For the great snowy owl had seen the weasel the moment he came into the woods, and recognized him as the enemy who had robbed her of the young owlets. On crept the weasel, feeling rather cross, when suddenly his little red eyes lighted upon four very peculiar tussocks of snow just beside a great log; and could he believe his eyes?—one of the snow bundles moved. Then the weasel knew there must be something hidden there. He stole nearer. He was in great luck; surely there were partridges there asleep in the snow. Instantly he gathered himself for a swift spring, but just as he was about to seize the first partridge, a great, white shadowy form, which might have been a giant snowflake, so silently did it fall, came swooping down upon the weasel from above, and the next instant the strong yellow talons hidden in the snowy feathers were buried in the weasel's fur, and he was lifted and borne in triumph through the air, twisting and struggling to gain his freedom, but vainly.

Then at a signal the brave leader of the partridges rose, and the other three went "whir, whir, whirring" off into the safe places of the forest.

XVIII

HOW SOLOMON OWL BECAME WISE

SOLOMON was the largest, as well as the most headstrong youngster in the screech-owl family. There were five of them, and they all lived in the knot-hole of a large sycamore tree down in the swamp. Just as soon as Solomon got through his pin-feather age, he began to show off and assert his independence. He would so bully the others, and jostle them about so roughly, that when the old owls came home with food for them, it always happened that the round, chuckle-head of Solomon managed to fill the knot-hole door, and always his greedy beak would snatch the forthcoming morsel from the others; for so furiously did he beat the little ones back, he always managed to get the very choicest bits.

Small wonder then that Solomon grew strong and lusty long before the others were out of their down and pin-feather age. Bold too and fearless he soon became, and when the purple twilight shadows began to deepen in the forest away down below him, Solomon would steal from the nest and sit blinking his beautiful yellow eyes until their black centers would expand from a mere dot, gradually growing larger, until all the daytime blindness had left him, and he could see everything about him. He saw the little brown bats, who slept all day, clinging like velvet bags to the limb of a tree, and each night he saw them unhook their claws, just at twilight, and dart squeaking away into the shadows after gnats. Then down below between dark, still aisles of the pines, night life in the forest began, and first of all a sly old lynx, with such an ugly disposition that he snarled at everything which crossed his path, would go skulking off by himself. Other night prowlers followed his example, and Solomon, watching them from his lofty perch, would suddenly unfurl his strong, young wings, with a swish as of rustling silk, and launch himself forth into the night.

Oh, it was wonderful to be free, and best of all, alone, for no longer did greedy Solomon have to share his food with the family. He knew instinctively where to hunt, and haunted the brooks and waterways for young frogs, who loved to come out of the water and sit upon the broad, cool lily pads enjoying the fragrance of snowy lilies which floated upon the water, as they sang their jolly choruses beneath the summer moon. Then down among the silvery ripples of the brook swam great shoals of little tender minnows, and into the tall sedges Solomon would dart like a flash, to snap up some trembling little field-mouse, or sleeping bird, who nested in the reedy marshes. Seldom did the yellow eyes or strong beak and talons of Solomon fail him, and soon he became famous among his wild kindred as a mighty hunter.

Now there are always certain things which young owls should know, and Mother Owl had tried to impress upon her children that they must always get back to the home nest before the sun rose and peeped above the top of the mountain, for, said she:

"Should you stay away from home after sunrise, you will never find your way back again, because you will be overtaken by the terrible sun blindness, and then you'll be as blind as a bat, and everybody knows how helpless and blind a bat is in the daytime, for they have to cover up their eyes with their wings all day long." All the other little owls listened respectfully to their mother's warning words, but Solomon just snapped his beak saucily at her, and blinked his great eyes quite indifferently at her advice, which had simply gone into one feathery ear and straight out of the other; secretly, he made up his mind then and there, that he would have an astonishing adventure. He would stay out and keep awake all day long, instead of coming back home with the others and going to sleep.

So one night Solomon flew off, as usual, alone, upon a hunting trip; a new, strange wildness possessed him, and he longed for adventures. He would fly off a long distance to new hunting grounds. High and low he soared, searching for prey, skimming low over strange, unexplored pools far from home; but somehow that night the moon shone so brightly that the frogs always saw him first, and down they would plunge, out of sight beneath the thick jungles of the water weeds, throwing back to him a defiant "kerchung." Finally Solomon realized to his dismay that night was almost gone, for the moon had disappeared behind a mountain, and still he had caught nothing to eat but just a few stray gnats. So he instantly made up his mind that it would be foolish to go back home

SOLOMON FAILED TO SEE THE TRAP

hungry, and perhaps when the big yellow sun ball actually came from behind the mountain, where it slept all night, then he would be able to find something quite different to eat, some new delicacy, for, with *more* light, he would certainly be able to see very much farther, instead of becoming blind like a stupid bat. He determined to stay awake and test it all for himself. Accordingly, back and forth he gaily flew over the gradually lightening marshes. And just as he was beginning to get fiercely hungry, he suddenly spied a choice morsel of fresh meat lying right in plain sight near the brook. Headlong, down swept Solomon, and grabbed the coveted bait greedily, so eagerly that he failed to see the trap beneath it, until it had nipped his leg and held him firmly, a prisoner.

Solomon soon found out that the more he flopped and struggled about to get free, the harder did the cruel teeth of the trap bite into his leg; so, finally, he had to lie with outstretched, helpless wings upon the trap. Meantime, higher and higher crept the daylight into the sky, and finally out burst the big, hot sun in a great blaze, and the higher it mounted into the sky the greater became poor, foolish Solomon's blindness. To add to his misery, the choice morsel of bait which he coveted, lay just outside his reach, and the trap bit and bit into his leg hotly.

In spite of his torment, Solomon began to know that unusual, daytime things, were going on all around him. Muskrats were taking their morning swim, splashing about in the water, and slapping their tails; birds, of which he knew nothing, sang beautiful, unfamiliar songs over his head. Thousands of sleeping gnats awoke and swarmed in the air, humming shrilly, while huge, lace-winged dragon-flies whirred close to his ears, and Solomon clicked his beak angrily at them as they swept past him. Then, to add to his misery, a whole drove of impudent little brown birds spied him, and began to tease and torment him. They would settle upon a near-by twig, then dart down upon him with little hateful "cheep, cheep, cheeps" of derision, flaunting their free wings saucily close to his half-blind eyes. Solomon beat his wings frantically to scare them off, but always they came back again to torment him. Next, a colony of crows came to drink at the brook and "caw, caw, caw'd" jeeringly at him; and all the time the hot sun beat down upon him and scorched and blinded him, so that he had to cover his eyes with their filmy lids, and defend himself as best he might. All day long Solomon endured the dreadful torments of daylight; then, when he was almost ready to give up, something happened.

"Pad, pad, pad," came the sound of stealthy footfalls, and then right through the tall cat-tails and sedges came slyly Red-Brush, the fox; jauntily he made his way toward the trap, for his keen, pointed snout had caught the fresh meat scent. Picking his way cautiously over the brook stones he came, lightly leaping across to the trap. Red-Brush saw Solomon and bared all his sharp, white teeth, in a grin of joy and anticipation. But first of all he would eat the bait, then finish off with the young owl later. With a great bound he was on the trap, and instantly, with this the eight teeth of the trap were sprung apart, and Solomon's leg was free. Then, even before Red-Brush could drop the bait, with a swift uprushing of wings Solomon was far above his head, and quite safe.

Solomon flew swiftly to the top of a lofty pine, and there beneath a limb, screened by dark, thick tufts of needles he sat alone and pondered. His foot was lame and stiff, and as daylight still lingered he blinked and winked to keep out the light. At last the hateful sun slipped away somewhere out of sight, and Solomon's blindness began to leave him, and he saw with joy the moon, pale and yellow, come creeping back to its place once more. He recognized the swift, shadowy forms of his neighbors, the bats, flitting about again. And then poor, lonely Solomon, unable to contain himself any longer, for sheer homesickness sent forth a wonderful call of misery and longing, out into the night.

"Who-ooo-o-o, who-ooo-o-o," he quavered, over and over again, and then before the last long "who-ooo-o-o" had fairly died away, away off somewhere over the tops of the tall pines came back an answering call, another "who-ooo," and Solomon heard and recognized it as it came nearer and nearer.

So, unfurling his soft, moth-like wings Solomon flew off in the direction of the familiar call, and was soon lost in the darkness of the forest. Thus did Solomon return to his home and kindred in the knot-hole of the sycamore tree, and never after that did he stay out all night, or until daylight, and thereafter he became known to all the little wild dwellers of the woods as a very wise owl.

XIX

THE KING OF BALSAM SWAMP

EVEN by day it was dark, lonely, and scary down in the Balsam Swamp, right under the frowning shadow of the mountain, and so wild that only an occasional cranberry picker ventured down into the marsh when the berries were ripe and red. Most people gave the lonely place a very wide berth, for it is easy to lose one's way in such a wilderness. So only the little wild creatures of the forest really knew very much about the many interesting inhabitants who lived in the swamp.

The little black bears came scrambling and sliding down from Porcupine Ridge occasionally to feed upon crawfish and frogs, and to wallow in the ooze and mud of the marsh, and when the red deer were hard pressed, and the hounds were baying close behind them, they found a safe hiding-place among the densely growing balsams. Thousands of the pointed green spires of the pine arose from the swamp, for the trees which grew there never had been chopped down by lumbermen. And so, if you only knew, the swamp was not, after all, such a lonely place, for many there were who loved it, and found a very safe home right there in the marsh.

Just over in the great black birch lived a very old raccoon and his interesting family; so old was this raccoon that he actually had rheumatism, and was quite gray in the face. The old raccoon could tell you many an exciting experience he had met with down in the swamp; how he had been chased by dogs and men, nights, when he had gone out to forage, how, when the hounds were baying, close upon his scent, he had cunningly doubled upon his track, crossed a brook many times, and so thrown them completely off the scent, leaving them to flounder and whine in the soft mud of the marshes while he had shinned up the great black birch in safety, and lying out flat upon a limb, actually grinned at the foolish hounds, showing all his little sharp white teeth for joy as they bayed and howled beneath the wrong tree.

Just beneath the great birch, in a dense clump of balsams, a young mother doe had come with her little dappled, frightened fawn, when the hunters were after them, and the mother's leg had been hurt. And the thick balsams and hemlocks hid them well, and the gray mosses and pine-needles beneath made a soft thick bed for them, and there they stayed until the danger was over and the doe was able to travel once more.

Up aloft, in the tall swaying tops of the pines, whole colonies of squirrels, red and gray, lived with the birds, for there was plenty of good food in the swamp: small, sweet beechnuts, and wild cherries with a puckery tang, and sweet nutty pits. Then there were bobcats, who snarled and howled and spit at each other in the dark nights, and an old Canadian lynx with sharp, tufted ears, and the ugliest disposition, for he snarled at everything which crossed his tracks.

Down beneath the low-lying branches of the spruces which swept the ground, forming regular tents, crept and grunted the stupid hedgehog family, grubbing for nuts and fresh water clams and crawfish, and bristling their sharp quills indignantly when any one presumed to disturb them; even at the gentle partridge family, who loved to cuddle in bunches beneath the green, tent-like branches, and then the brave little cock partridge would ruffle up his feathers and rush out upon the hedgehogs furiously with a "whir-r-r-r," and a drumming commotion, which often startled the lazy hedgehogs out of their wits, so that they would roll over in sudden terror and bristle out their quills until they looked like a round ball of sharp needles. Well the hedgehog knew that no enemy would care to come very near him then, lest they get a snout full of sharp quills.

If the Balsam Swamp was a creepy, dark place in the daytime, at night it was ten times more fearsome, for then every wild dweller in the depths of the swamp awoke, and the place was filled with strange sounds. The first signal for all to begin stirring in the swamp was given by the frogs who began their evening chorus, "Zoom, zoom, kerchung, kerchung," down in the bogs. Just as soon as the old raccoon heard the first "zoom, zoom" of the old giant bullfrog, he hastily began to scratch and claw himself up out of his hole in the black birch, where he had been sleeping all day long. Next, the snarling lynx glided like a shadow from his lair, and went, with soft, velvet-padded footsteps, skulking off between the thick balsams after his prey; and then something else happened. For when it was just about dark enough, from right in the very heart of the marsh the King of the swamp sent out his lonely, blood-curdling cry: "Who-ho-ho, who-ho-ho-ho-ho-ho." It was the great white owl, the very oldest inhabitant of the swamps; a regular old hermit was this great snowy owl, and he lived all alone in a giant pine, which had long ago been blasted by lightning. The pine towered over all the spire-like tops of the balsams and spruces of the marsh; white and lonely looking it stretched its blasted, crooked limbs forth like the arms of some great forest giant.

The trunk of the old pine was hollow, and deep within the whitened depths of this tree lived the King. Alone, despised, and forsaken by his mate and all his kindred, because of his fierce, vindictive temper, and shunned by all his furry neighbors also, because the sly old King had a way of knowing just where to find young baby raccoons when their mother was away; and he would even carry off a very young lynx cub, if he chanced to be pressed by hunger, while nothing delighted him more than to steal like a shadow upon a covey of sleeping partridges and scatter then like leaves, taking his pick of the family, and when the angry little father bravely "whirr'd and whirr'd," the King was not at all frightened; for nothing ever daunted him very much.

Silently, on his great, soft white wings, he swooped down upon any tender little furry creature that chanced to come in sight of his great, staring yellow eyes, and then with one cruel blow of his lance-like beak he killed his prey and carried it swiftly off in his great horny talons to the old blasted pine in the heart of the swamp.

Only once or twice had the King been caught napping. That was when he made a great mistake and tried to rob the farmer's muskrat trap, and the steel teeth had caught and nipped off one of his great horny toes, so that ever after that time he always hated the very sight of a muskrat, and never troubled them. Another time the King had a hard fight with a great blue heron. He had tried to take away a fish from the heron for which it had been fishing a long, long time, and somehow the heron's long, sharp bill had punctured one of the King's great, yellow eyes. Since his encounter with the heron, the King's sight had not been so keen, and sometimes, when weary, or on a long flight, he flew with sideway motion.

Far up on a lofty ledge of the mountain which overhung the swamp, two bald eagles made their lonely, untidy nest every year, and raised their scrawny brood of young eaglets. The old eagles were faithful creatures, and looked out well for the wants of their young, never thinking of themselves at any time, so that they could get food enough to fill the wide-open, hungry mouths of their screaming little ones. It was simply wonderful how much the young eaglets ate to satisfy their hunger; for they managed to keep the old birds flying about for food from earliest daylight until the frogs began their evening song down in the marsh.

Very well the old King of the swamp knew of the eagles' nest. He also knew just when the young eaglets were left lying alone in their nest, for at the early hour when the old eagles were forced to leave the ledge, the King was occasionally awake himself, especially if he himself had come home from his night's wanderings hungry.

Once it happened that very, very early in the morning the King came back to the pine in a very bad humor, for he had been out all night long hunting for food, and he had found nothing worth eating.

"Who, ho, ho, ho-ho, ho-ho," he grumbled to himself crossly. "Not a bite to eat all night." Perhaps the old owl's eyes were less keen than formerly. Nothing left for him to prey upon but hedgehogs. "Lazy things! Who wants to put their eyes out trying to eat a hedgehog?" thought the King. "Who, ho, ho-ho," he croaked.

Just then he chanced to cock up one of his great eyes toward the ledge in time to see two dark shadowy forms hover over the edge. The old eagles were making a very early start for food for the eaglets.

Instantly the King was wide awake and alert; he waited only until the two dark shadows had passed out of sight over the mountain, then, silently, on his great, soft white wings he rose and rose in the air until level with the ledge, when he darted down and, seizing a young eaglet in his talons, was back to the pine again before the old eagles came back.

What a screaming and commotion took place when the old eagles returned and found one of their brood missing; but the old King cared little for this, for, having satisfied his pressing hunger, he was by this time safely hidden down inside the hollow pine, fast asleep.

The very next time the King happened to return home hungry after a night out, he instantly remembered about the young eagles. True enough, the one he had eaten had been exceedingly tough; but then, when one is hungry, young eagle is better than nothing at all. So, with his great golden eyes wide open and watching eagerly, he soon had the satisfaction of seeing the old eagles leave the nest and start forth in the early dawn; first one eagle arose from the ledge, flying straight over the mountain, then the mate soon followed after, and before she was fairly out of sight, unable to wait longer, for he was very hungry, swiftly the old King rose in the air to the eagles' ledge.

"Screech, screech," shrilled the young eaglets, and just then the old King's maimed talon lost its grip of the young bird which he had selected, for young eaglets are strong, which made the youngsters screech still louder. Again the King's horny talon gripped the eaglet, and so very much taken up was he, and so very hungry, that he utterly failed to see the shadow of a pair of wide wings gradually hovering, hovering, drawing closer to the ledge with every movement, until, with a sudden sound as of rustling silk, the wings wavered and dropped straight down from above, and the great lance-like talons of the enraged mother eagle were buried in the snowy back of the King, even before he had a chance to turn about and face her.

Then a mighty battle began between the mother eagle and the old King of the swamp. They finally cleared the ledge together, and went swirling out into space. Feathers of white and brown fell in showers, and floated down into the marsh, as they fought on and on, with great beaks snapping sharply, the eagle screaming weirdly, occasionally, as they battled in the air.

But the old King of the swamp had met his match at last, for the mother eagle well knew that she was fighting to the death the one who had robbed her nest before. In vain did the King seek to gain his home nest in the blasted pine. The eagle stuck to him, tearing at him cruelly with beak and talons until, finally, fluttering weakly, utterly exhausted, his spirit broken, blind and dying, the King began to fall. Fluttering weakly he began to settle down, down into a dark, hidden spot beneath the thick balsams. He had become just a mere bundle of snowy feathers now; all fierceness had departed, and there was nothing left of the King for the little wild things of the forest to longer fear and hate.

And that night when the frogs started off with their usual signal, calling all to awaken in the marshes, the "Who, ho, ho-ho, ho-ho, o-o" of the old King of the swamp was silent.

XX

THE GIANT OF THE CORN-FIELD

DAME WOODCHUCK, old and decrepit, came to the entrance of her burrow and peered anxiously forth, for she always poked the very tip of her brown nose out first, and then, if she happened to find the coast quite clear, she would venture to waddle entirely out.

Poor old thing, so old and covered with fat that she could not travel far; besides, one hind leg had once been caught in a steel trap and lamed, so that now she was almost doubly helpless. Her thick fur coat was of a dull reddish brown, and very much faded by sun and rain, and so badly worn off in certain places it looked really moth-eaten, while her black snout and stiff whiskers were quite gray with age.

Dame Woodchuck had very wisely selected her home, for you might stroll right past the great clump of rank nettles where it was, a hundred times without even suspecting that it concealed the door to a woodchuck's burrow, because, you see, the vines of a wild woodbine trailed over the nettles, and formed such a fine curtain that it quite concealed the entrance to her home.

Of course all the little wild dwellers of the woods and her neighbors, who always know about such secret dwellings, might have told you where old Dame Woodchuck actually lived, but then, you see, they never did.

It was a bright, sunny day, and Dame Woodchuck enjoyed sitting in the door of her home, for the pleasant sun felt very grateful as it shone warmly down upon her aching old back. Besides, it was pleasant to chat with the neighbors who occasionally passed that way. After ascertaining, beyond a doubt, that her most dreaded enemy, the farmer's yellow dog, whom she detested greatly because he delighted to pounce out upon her suddenly and worry and torment her, was nowhere in sight, with much wheezing and little chattering complaints, Dame Woodchuck managed to flop out of her burrow and sitting bolt upright upon her haunches, just in the brown, upturned earth in front of the nettle patch, she watched and waited for the return of her dilatory son, Ichabod. To tell the truth, the Dame was really beginning to feel a bit angry and out of patience with him, and well she might, for she was very, very hungry, and as she was now too old and lame to go off any distance to forage for herself she had to depend almost entirely upon Ichabod for food. Long had she been anticipating his return with the juicy, yellow turnips which he had been sent to bring from the farmer's garden, where each year they grew so plentifully. What could have become of Ichabod? How tiresome to have to wait such a long, long while. Ichabod had been gone long enough to go to the garden and back twice over.

As Dame Woodchuck sat waiting for the turnips, pleasant recollections of bygone days suddenly came into her mind, days when the woodchuck family had been a large and happy one. Well she remembered the time when she and her mate had dug their burrow close to the beautiful field of pink clover, where every morning all the little woodchucks used to spend hours rolling and tumbling about in the fragrant, dew-laden blossoms.

What wonderful happiness had been theirs. But alas! to her sorrow, the farmer had found their burrow and broken up the happy family. One by one all the children had been caught in traps, until now but Ichabod remained of her five little ones. And then, worst blow of all, her mate, evidently faithless, had gone off and left them. Shortly after that the beautiful clover field had all been plowed up, and now it lay in ugly brown furrows, bare, unlovely, and as Dame Woodchuck looked back into the pleasant past a tear of grief and regret stole into her bleary eyes and trickled down her gray, furry cheeks.

Suddenly the Dame heard a scuffling, scuttling sound among the ferns, and then she speedily forgot all her sad thoughts, and was instantly alert, and listening with her small round ears. It was Ichabod. With a grunt of welcome and satisfaction she accepted eagerly, and fell to munching hungrily, the hard, unripe apple which he had brought to her. However, she felt far from satisfied with the apple, for she had all this time been anticipating the turnip, and the apple was so sour she did not relish it very keenly. Still, it was perhaps better than nothing at all. Ichabod had a strange story to tell, and the Dame listened with dismay as he told her that the farmer had planted no turnips in his garden this season. Evidently Ichabod had brought to his mother the very best he could find. But Ichabod brought also strange news.

A friendly raccoon, whom he had met during his absence, had told him quite a wonderful tale: that across the cranberry bogs, far over on the other side of the great hill covered with the pointed balsam firs, which lay in plain sight of the burrow, might be found a pleasant valley, and best of all in the valley was a great field of young corn. Already the plumy blades were beginning to bend down, heavy with their weight of milky sweet corn, upon whose juicy kernels one might live in luxury until the frost came, for not until then would the corn be harvested by the farmer.

Moreover, between the sentinel-like corn-stalks great golden pumpkins were fast ripening. Oh, what a land of plenty! If one were only there upon the enchanted ground. Dame Woodchuck gazed disconsolately and impatiently forth at the dreary prospect which lay spread out before her nettle-draped door and pondered over her situation. She knew that a time of action had arrived in the woodchuck family, and that she and Ichabod must surely go forth and seek a new home at last.

So that very night, when the great yellow moon rose over the dark hills, the Dame left her old burrow and waddled forth, with Ichabod following closely behind, to find a new home where food should be plentiful.

Across the perilous deep morasses of the cranberry bogs she dragged her unwieldy old body. Necessarily they traveled quite slowly, for the way seemed long and difficult, and the poor old thing was weak from lack of proper food. Often they paused in their night journey to rest and enjoy their new surroundings, for the Dame had never traveled very far from her old burrow before. Down in the thickets of the cranberry bog the whippoorwills sang plaintively their tremulous song; the Dame and Ichabod listened, and heard also, occasionally, the sleepy call of a nesting hermit thrush down in the meadows. Sometimes a hoot owl would brush past them, and call at them jeeringly. On the edge of the marshes they came into a great bed of dewy clover, sweet and cool. Here they paused to rest and feed.

Finally they reached the open country, and in the distance, in the moonlight, they plainly distinguished the tall wavy shadows of the corn of which the kind raccoon had told them. They had reached the promised land of plenty at last.

Very fortunately for the Dame and Ichabod they chanced to come across a deserted rabbit hole, which by a little judicious digging they very soon converted into quite a comfortable home; so that before any of the other little wild creatures in that neighborhood were awake the next morning the Dame and Ichabod had taken possession of their new burrow and were soon fast asleep in an upper chamber.

As Dame Woodchuck was so very weary and lame from her long journey she could not travel far from her home, but had to content herself at first with simply dragging herself to the door of the burrow, where she would gaze forth long and hopefully at the new and pleasant prospect spread out before her tired old eyes.

There, sure enough, not many fields away, lay the beautiful corn-field, where already choice ears filled with tender grains, just suited to her worn old teeth, were waiting, to be had for the taking, and she knew that already Ichabod was in the field, scurrying about beneath the wavy green plumes.

Great was the alarm and dismay of the Dame when Ichabod finally returned to her with no food and a strange fearsome tale of what had happened to him upon his first visit to the corn. It was all true enough about the fine, juicy corn; it was there, and plenty of it for everybody, just as the kind raccoon had told them. But, unfortunately, the whole field was ruled over, watched and guarded by a frightful monster, who occupied a commanding position right in the very center of the corn-field, where he guarded well the corn both by night and day; with angry, menacing mien he stood there, and no one dare intrude. Moreover, Solomon Crow and his family, who sat upon a rail fence near the corn-field, had told a terrible tale of certain unseen snares placed for the unwary, which the terrible creature had spread out all about him. Many of the crows had been caught in the innocent appearing threads, had given a few futile flops and strident caws, and that had been the last of them.

Oh, the giant who guarded the corn was indeed a fearful monster. Built upon similar lines to the farmer himself, whom they had all often seen, but far, far more horrible to look upon was this creature of the corn-field, who towered far above the tallest corn-stalks and held leveled at intruders an unknown weapon, from which fluttered yards and yards of fearsome streaming objects, and when the wind blew across the field the creature who guarded the corn shook with rage from top to toe. The giant's hair was ragged and unkempt, and bristled forth fiercely from beneath his tattered old hat. Ichabod, somewhat bolder than others, wishing to get a full view, had crept as closely as he dared, and rising upon his hind legs, by the aid of a stone, he had stolen one fleeting glance full at the giant of the corn-field. One look had been quite sufficient for Ichabod and had sent him, panic-stricken with fear, hustling away; so hastily did he travel that he left a large tuft of his fur in a barb-wire fence beneath which he slid, and ran scuttling back home to his mother with chattering teeth.

Now Dame Woodchuck was very old and wise in experience, and she had in her long lifetime heard of such giants as Ichabod told her he had seen in the corn-field. And never in all her life had she ever heard of one of the creatures harming a woodchuck, in spite of gossip. After all, the crows were mostly gossips. It was certainly high time that Ichabod began to learn a few lessons from life, and have more courage and responsibility. Besides, the more the Dame thought of the luscious sweet corn so close at hand, the more hungry did she become.

So finally, quite unable to endure the trying situation longer, Dame Woodchuck herself started forth to investigate the matter. And Ichabod, not wishing to tarry home alone, ran along beside his old mother. They often stopped to rest and chat by the roadside, and all the terrifying stories which they heard of the giant filled them with secret dismay. But Dame Woodchuck was very brave at heart and did not lose her courage easily. So skirting the edge of the corn-field they soon gained a little hillock, where they had a full view of the monster. It was only too true; there he stood, undaunted and firm, waving aloft his fluttering, terrifying warning. Dame Woodchuck and Ichabod sat bolt upright upon their haunches and stared at the creature with bulging eyes.

Just at that very moment a deafening bang sounded, and a great cloud of smoke arose from the vicinity of the giant, and the next moment Peter Rabbit, with a wild cry of warning, dashed past them in mad haste, running for his very life. In an instant Dame Woodchuck and Ichabod had dropped down flat upon their stomachs and there they lay trembling together beneath a great bunch of burdock leaves. Perhaps even now the giant was searching about among the corn for them. They waited until their courage returned and finally crept back home again, quite sadly disappointed, for they had not even been able to taste a kernel of corn.

The situation in the woodchuck home was, after this, rather a desperate one, for food was again becoming scarce. How aggravating, too, when the luscious corn was ripening almost within sight of their door.

Dame Woodchuck's sides soon became quite flabby, so that her fur coat actually hung in plaits and ridges upon her back, so loose did it become, while her eyes fairly bulged with anxiety and discouragement.

" 'Tis always darkest before dawn," as the saying goes, and already brighter days were in store for the Dame and Ichabod.

One dark night, when they were fast asleep in their snug burrow, they were suddenly awakened in the middle of the night by a terrific rumbling and crashing above their heads. This frightful commotion and din went on all night long, and cowardly Ichabod squeaked and shook with fear, and crept close to his mother's side.

"Lie still, O timorous one," said his mother, trying to quiet him. "Do not be afraid; 'tis but the great Storm Spirit. He is passing this way." By morning the commotion had ceased, and then Ichabod and his mother ventured to peer forth from their door. And what a sight was that which greeted their eyes. Great trees of the forest now lay prone upon the ground, which the mighty Storm Spirit in his strength had laid low everywhere in passing, for he had left ruin in his wake.

And then Peter Rabbit scurried past their door, and paused long enough to tell them some great and glorious good news, which was, that the mighty Storm Spirit had actually destroyed their great enemy, the terrible giant of the corn-field. At last the terrible creature had been conquered, and now lay prone and helpless upon the ground, a terror no longer to the little timid wild creatures who wore fur and feathers.

Already the crows were cawing the news triumphantly over his remains and feasting meantime greedily upon the unguarded corn, and then, very soon the Dame and Ichabod had joined them, and were burying their sharp teeth hungrily in the milky sweet kernels of corn. For the reign of the corn giant was now at an end, and soon Dame Woodchuck and her son became very,

very plump and sleek, and fine and strong. And when the autumn winds began to blow chill and keen, and Jack Frost came and froze over all the little brooks and waterways, then they withdrew into their snug burrow for the winter, as they always do, and after stuffing up the entrance of their door securely with leaves and earth, that the snow might not drift and filter inside, there they slumbered together, comfortable and warm, until it was time to come out in the spring to see if they could find their shadows; for the woodchucks know best of any of the little forest creatures when spring is actually come.

XXI

THE BRAVERY OF EBENEZER COON

"De raccoon tail am ringed all 'roun."

Once, a long time ago, there lived in an old oak tree in the middle of a deep forest, a large family of raccoons. In due course of time all the little ones grew up, and choosing mates, as is their custom, one after the other they deserted the old home tree until finally the only remaining one was Ebenezer. Ebenezer so loved the deep, comfortable nest, hollowed out far down in the trunk of the oak tree, that he preferred to stay right there instead of going out into the world with his brothers and sisters and finding a new home.

So there he lived all alone and in time he became known as a sort of a hermit. Ebenezer was really a fine, handsome fellow, with a black, pointed snout and stiffly bristling whiskers, deep, yellowish-brown fur, expressive, meditative green eyes, and small, alert, round ears, and when he moved about, or the wind blew across his fat back, his fur was so long and fine that it actually waved. But most remarkable of all Ebenezer's many attractions was, perhaps, his fine, plume-like tail, of which he was inordinately vain.

Now Ebenezer Coon took what might be called "solid comfort." The baying hounds never molested him, for just beneath and all around his home tree grew a perfect battlement of thorn bush, and often Ebenezer, from a safe retreat in some abandoned squirrel's nest, would peek cautiously over its edge and with little rumbling grunts of satisfaction and fun he would watch the baffled hounds who had scented his retreat, while they gave up the chase in disgust, backing out with torn, bleeding ears and cruel spikes from the thorn bush piercing their inquisitive snouts.

One night, just as the big, yellow moon arose from behind the dark mountains, and its rays began to penetrate and filter through the thick dark pines, Ebenezer awoke from his customary, all-day sleep and began to pull himself up out of his nest. He dearly loved to go abroad on a moonlight night, enjoying the scenery while he leisurely foraged about for food. Having clawed his way up out of his hole he took up his position on a flat limb of the pine, gazing forth over the prospect with approval, and turning over in his mind just what he should do that night.

The owls were already out, hooting and calling soft answers back and forth to each other, and hermit thrushes were still singing their plaintive lullabies drowsily, in the thorn thickets, while down in the marshes the frogs and peepers had already begun their nightly serenade. Occasionally, from far off over the mountain, a whippoorwill called lonesomely. Even the bats were out foraging, for the soft night moths which they loved to hunt on the wing, and flapped, squeaking shrilly, close to Ebenezer's head.

Ebenezer felt lazy, and began to stretch out first one black, claw-tipped foot, then the other, yawning and showing all his little sharp white teeth. At last he was quite awake and instantly began to realize that he was frightfully hungry. His pressing needs soon set his sluggish wits to work and he began to think longingly of a far-away field of ripening corn. True, the corn was a long distance from home, but Ebenezer never bothered about distances when he went hunting for sweet corn. It was the one dainty in all the world for which he cared most.

Now the more he thought about the milk-white, ripening kernels of corn, encased in their pale green, silken husks, the hungrier did Ebenezer become, until, unable to endure the situation longer, with sudden, desperate haste he began to slide and claw his way down the trunk of the oak tree. Ebenezer was now in fine spirits, for the night was simply perfect, and just suited his plans, so he frolicked along the forest path, often giving little ridiculous skips and bounds into the air for sheer joy. He skirted a deep ravine, then crossed the brook where he paused to dip his black snout into the bubbles, scattering a shoal of silvery minnows leaping and playing in the water.

Just before Ebenezer reached the corn-field he came across a queer, round bundle, or ball, lying directly in his path. Ebenezer never turned out for anything which happened to be in his road. He was far too indolent to do that—he always waited for others to make way for him. So he kept right on, and when he came close to the queer ball he playfully decided to see if it was alive, and have some fun with it. He reached forth, rather gingerly at first, and touched the thing with the tip of his paw. It did not move, so then he commenced to jostle it rudely about with his black snout. Just as he was beginning to rather enjoy the game, all of a sudden the supposed ball suddenly unrolled itself, stood upright and charged savagely at him. And then before Ebenezer knew it, he had been bowled over on his fat back, with his nose and cheeks stuck full of cruel sharp quills. The supposed ball had simply been a stray porcupine who had rolled himself up into a neat ball and gone to sleep.

Without stopping to even glance at poor Ebenezer, the porcupine, having revenged himself for being disturbed, turned and waddled back into the forest, grunting indignantly to himself as he traveled.

"Gar-r-r-r, gar-r-r-r," snarled Ebenezer in a perfect frenzy of agony and rage, lifting his fore paws to his smarting cheeks and trying vainly to pull out the sharp, barbed quills which were penetrating his flesh. But he soon found out that the more he rubbed and scratched, the worse the cruel quills hurt him.

"Gar-r-r-r, gar-r-r-r," howled Ebenezer again, more loudly and impatiently than before. Just then a white cottontail rabbit chanced to be passing that way, and heard the agonized cries of the poor raccoon and instantly saw what had happened, for once one of her own family had encountered a porcupine.

"Friend Raccoon, you seem to be in trouble," said the kind rabbit, in the language in which the little wild creatures of the forest converse together. "Pray, let me help you, for I understand just exactly what to do."

So saying, the white rabbit, with her soft little paws, deftly removed the cruel needles from the raccoon's face, and then bidding him seek for a mullein leaf covered with night dew, and apply it to his smarting wounds, she left him.

Of course Ebenezer was most grateful to the kind rabbit for her timely aid, and he then and there made up his mind that if ever it lay in his power to repay the rabbit's kindness he would go out of his way to do so. Then Ebenezer, after satisfying his hunger with corn, went back to his home, and rolling himself into a fur ball, went to sleep.

In spite of the fact that Ebenezer was indolent and lazy by nature, he possessed one very commendable trait of character. He was extremely neat and dainty in all his habits, and never dreamed of tasting a morsel of food which he might chance to find until he had first given it a thorough washing, whatever the food might be, if a turnip, an ear of corn or a land crab. Just as soon as Ebenezer found it he would always hurry away to the nearest pool and thoroughly rinse it before he ate it.

Some time after his adventure with the porcupine, he happened to be out hunting for food. Now there had been a great freshet in the land at that time, so food was very scarce and many of the little wild things had lost their lives, or been driven from their homes along the banks of the brook by the mighty, rushing waters. Of course the raccoon was quite safe, for his home nest was high above the freshet. Ebenezer chanced upon a floating corn-stalk that day, on which he was delighted to find an ear of corn. It was a lucky find for the hungry raccoon, and, very happy about it, he hastily stripped off the husk and leaning over the stream began to rinse the ear of corn in the water. Just as he had decided that it was properly rinsed, and that he might as well eat it, he suddenly heard a cry of fear and agony, and looking up-stream, he saw a strange sight.

Borne upon the rushing, muddy waters of the freshet he saw a log, and upon it were three little white rabbits. They were clinging frantically to the log, which came whirling swiftly on down-stream. Just below thundered and roared the falls, and should they plunge over them they must surely perish. Ebenezer saw their danger. At the same instant he also realized that now had come the opportunity to show forth his gratitude for the rabbit's kindness to him.

That very instant the log swerved and was caught and held fast by the branch of a tree. Oh, would the branch hold it? With quick, bold strokes Ebenezer plunged straight into the roaring, rushing waters, and swam quickly out to the log. He realized, however, that he could never reach the shore again if the rabbits clung to his wet body and hampered his movements in the water, so instantly he told them just what to do.

"Quick, seize hold of my tail and hang on for dear life," called Ebenezer to the first little rabbit. And then with the little, frightened thing clinging desperately to his plumy tail, Ebenezer swam quickly to the shore and left it and returning twice again, he succeeded in saving the last little helpless rabbit just as the log with a lunge went swirling down-stream.

Ebenezer Coon was very tired indeed after the rescue, and the last time he swam back to shore his fur was so heavy with water and the additional weight of the last little rabbit that it was all he could do to manage to reach the bank. So, faint and weary, for a while Ebenezer lay exhausted upon the bank, while the three little rabbits, after drying their fur in the sunshine, bade Ebenezer farewell and scurried back home to their mother.

After Ebenezer felt rested, he found his ear of corn again, nibbled a bit at it to stay his hunger, then dragged his tired body home, and clawing his way heavily up into the home tree, rolled himself up comfortably and slept.

Now all unbeknown to Ebenezer, while he slumbered, much excitement and gossip was taking place among all the little wild folk of the forest, for everybody was commenting upon the brave act of Ebenezer Coon in saving the three little white rabbits. And then the kind fairy of the woods, who watches and rewards all such little creatures for their good deeds and acts of bravery, especially, and knows everything which takes place in the animal kingdom, of course soon knew all about Ebenezer's bravery, therefore planned out a little surprise which should be his reward.

So when Ebenezer finally awoke from his long nap, and came out as usual to sit and sun himself upon his favorite limb in the oak tree, then all the little wild things saw at once when they looked upon Ebenezer Coon that he had indeed been rewarded for his bravery, because the raccoon's tail, which had always been just plain gray in color, like the rest of his coat, was now ringed about with five beautifully shaded jet-black rings—the decoration, the wonderful badge of distinction conferred on Ebenezer Coon for his bravery. And so ever since that time the beautiful, plumy tail of every raccoon in the kingdom has been marked with five jet-black rings.

XXII

THE NARROW ESCAPE OF VELVET WINGS

"WHIR, whir, whir," sounded the swish of many silken wings. The swallows had arrived from the South; thousands of them there were, long winged and dusky brown, with faintly russet breasts. So full of joyous bustle they were over their arrival, "cheep, cheep, cheeping," making a great clamor as they separated into colonies, seeking to locate for the summer. The old red barn seemed to invite them; in fact, two colonies had a regular pitched battle over its possession, until at last the stronger band drove away the weaker, and took possession of the coveted spot. They swarmed into the old barn through small windows high in its peak, chattering together as they selected building sites, many of them hastily using last season's mud-caked foundations. So great a disturbance did the swallows make in the silence of the dim, old barn that they disturbed and finally awakened many who had not aroused themselves from their winter's torpor and sleep.

Far up in a distant peak of the barn, in a certain dim corner, where a great rafter lapped, forming a secluded sort of shelf, there hung, stretched across the corner, an unusually large cobweb curtain. The old gray spider who had spun the web had abandoned his web when cold weather came, and crawled down into the warm hay. Gradually thick dust collected upon the web curtain, and well it did, because back of it, upon the wide, dusty beam it covered, lay two torpid things, resembling nothing so much as two round balls of brown fur.

The strident chatter of the swallows had penetrated the small round ears of the two fur balls, perhaps, or it might have been the light from a stray yellow sunbeam, which at a certain hour of each day had a way of filtering through a crack and warming their retreat. At any rate, one of the torpid things began to slowly undo itself; a small, mouse-like head appeared first, having round, delicate ears of membrane, which appeared rather too large for its head. Its eyes, when it opened them, were exactly like two black-jet beads, and its rather wide, pink mouth was liberally armed with tiny, saw-like teeth, which the fur ball showed as it yawned sleepily, stretching itself, and spreading out its wings, to which were attached by a thin membrance its forearms and legs. Then, fully awake, it plunged straight through the cobweb curtain, tearing it apart from end to end, and sending back a sharp, encouraging squeak to the smaller fur ball to follow.

Of course the two ridiculous fur balls were just the bat family, and lifelong tenants of the old red barn, as everybody knows. The smaller, more timorous bat, soon followed her mate from behind the web curtain and joined him upon the broad beam. But so clumsy and half awake was she that the very first thing she did was to make a misstep and go pitching off the high beam into space. She landed upon the hay, fortunately, and then began the funniest sight. Did you ever chance to see a bat when it attempted to walk? They seldom use their feet, and when they do it is a droll sight.

As soon as Mrs. Bat recovered from her dizzy fall, she put forth one wing and a hind leg and began to walk toward a beam, for strangely enough she could not fly from so low an elevation, but must climb some distance in order to launch herself properly into the air. Hitching and tumbling along she finally reached a beam, and clutching it she began to climb it head downward, exactly as a woodpecker does. Then, having reached the desired height, she whirled away, and landed finally beside her mate.

The barn was a very silent place. The rasping of its rusty latch always gave ample time for all its little wild tenants to get under cover, so usually all you heard when you entered would be the hidden, lonely trill of a cricket or a faint, stealthily rustle in the hay.

Upon a broad beam far up over the loft where the oat straw was stored, lived rather an exclusive family, that of the barn owl. You would never have dreamed they were there, so well did the brown feathers of the owls blend in with the dimness of the shadows. Under the grain bins, far down below, lived a large colony of fat rats, while in among the dried clover raced and romped shoals of field-mice who wintered there. But there was another, a new tenant, feared and shunned by all the others. He came from no one knew where, exactly; still the farmer's boy might have explained, for he had lost a pet ferret.

The ferret was an ugly creature to look upon, its body long and snaky, and covered with yellowish-white, rather dirty-looking fur; its movements were sly and furtive, and somehow always struck terror to every tenant of the barn whenever they saw him steal forth. All winter the ferret had been there, and the hay was literally honeycombed with its secret tunnels, and woe to anything which happened to cross its evil trail.

Each evening soon after twilight the swallows would return to the barn from their raids, and when the shadows grew quite dusky, far down beneath them, then the bats and the barn owl family would launch themselves out into the night.

"Squeak, squeak," ordered the big male bat; then like two shadows they would flit silently off upon their velvety wings. All during the early part of the night they chased gnats and bugs, because they invariably got their best pickings before midnight, for after that time insects were harder to find because most of them crawl beneath sheltering leaves, as the night wanes, to get away from the heavy, drenching dew, or hide from their enemies before daylight overtakes them. Before the dim shadows began to lift, the bats and owls had returned, usually, but the bat family did not retire again behind their cobweb curtain; instead they hung themselves by their wing claws head downward from their beam, folding their wings closely over their beady eyes, and thus they would sleep all day.

Warmer days came, and livelier times were stirring among the tenants of the barn. Far up on her own beam Mrs. Barn Owl tended and fed two young downy owlets faithfully. Of course the owl mother knew the beam to be quite a safe spot for baby owls, but somehow she distrusted the skulking old ferret, whom she occasionally caught sight of; besides, rats sometimes climb beams, and once, before the owl eggs had hatched, something had stolen one egg; so that is really why there were but *two* owlets instead of three.

The swallows were the busiest tenants imaginable, for each nest now held a circle of gaping, hungry mouths to feed. All day long, and far into twilight, the swallows were whirring incessantly, in and out. But up in the secret corner, partially hidden by the torn cobweb curtain, clung Mrs. Bat herself, and if you could only have peeped beneath one of her wings you might have seen the dearest little mite of a bat, with eyes of jet, clinging close to its mother's breast as she folded it tenderly beneath her wing. There the helpless little creature stayed, close to its mother, until it became older and stronger, for among all the tiny, fur-bearing animals there is no little mother more considerate of her young than the bat. And rather than leave the little furry thing all alone upon the great beam when she had to go off for food, as she could not carry it *beneath* her wing in flight, she would make a kind of little basket cradle by spreading out her wing, and thus the baby bat would ride with his mother, clinging close to her back with his wing hooks and tiny teeth, and he never fell from the wing basket nor was he afraid.

When the young owlets were out of the pin-feather stage they began to go out with the old ones. But once when they were left behind, sitting huddled together upon their beam, when the mother owl came back only one small, chuckle-faced owlet remained. Hunt as she might, the robber had left no clue behind. However, her suspicions centered upon the sly old ferret and she took to watching his movements more than ever. There she would sit, sullen and revengeful, far up among the shadows and beams, with her one owlet. She frequently saw the sinuous, snake-like body of the ferret creep forth, and even caught the sound of his peculiarly hateful hiss when he encountered anything in his path. Once, in a great fury she swooped clear down to the barn floor after her enemy, but she got there a second too late. The sly creature had heard the swish of the owl's wings when she left the beam, and caught a fleeting glimpse of her blazing yellow eyes, so he hastily slid into the nearest runway, and the owl flew back to her beam defeated; but she never forgot, she simply waited.

More and more bold became the raids of the hateful old ferret. He robbed the swallows' nests; frequently you might see his dirty-white, sinuous body stealing across some high beam, creeping, creeping, warily arching his back, holding his snaky head high, one foot gathered up, looking for an unguarded nest; then, if he found one, he would arch his snaky neck over the edge of the nest and suck every egg.

Velvet Wings, the young bat, grew very fast. He foraged for himself now, for his wings were as broad and fleet as his mother's. Sometimes, however, he made a clumsy start and so got many a fall. So one night as he started forth he fell fluttering and squeaking and protesting, until with a soft thud he landed far below upon the barn floor. Completely stunned Velvet Wings lay there, his wings outspread and helpless, his little heart beating so hard it shook his whole body. Of course he saw nothing, so did not notice the peaked snout of the sly old ferret as he peered inquisitively forth from his lair in the haymow to see what the soft thud might be. The next instant the ferret had Velvet Wings in his cruel mouth, but instead of devouring him at once he began to have some fun with the poor bat, tossing it in the air, then pouncing upon it as it fell, mauling it as a cat does a mouse, pinning its wings down with both fore feet. A second more and Velvet Wings would have been lost, but that second was not allowed the ferret; for far up among the brown rafters a pair of great, blazing yellow eyes had been watching, and like a rocket from above fell the old mother owl, clear to the barn floor. "Swish, swish," went her great wings, as she buried her talons in the back of the dirty-white fur coat. With a twist of his snaky, supple body, the ferret managed to free himself a second from that awful clutch, and arching its back, it began to slip away. But the owl was too quick; landing upon the ferret's back, she took another, firmer hold and bore him, struggling and snarling, aloft.

Down through the center of the old barn a broad sunbeam entered. It left a long bar of light through the dimness of the dusky place. The barn was strangely silent, hushed, but many bright eyes had witnessed the tragedy and were watching to see the end, but all that they finally saw was just a few wisps of white fur, which came floating lazily down through the bar of light. It appeared not unlike floating thistle-down, but it had come from the owl's nest, and was the last they ever saw of their enemy, the sly old ferret.

Up there in the dim shadows of the old red barn you'll find them all, and should the yellow beam of sunlight happen to dance across their dark hiding-place, you may plainly see the bat family. There they all hang through the day, looking for all the world like a row of small velvet bags, their bright eyes shrouded by their soft wings as they sleep, head downward; while off in quite another corner, perched upon her own dusty beam, drowses the brave barn owl and her one chuckle-headed owlet.

XXIII

NEMOX, THE CRAFTY ROBBER OF THE MARSHES

NEMOX, the fisher, who lived in the hollow of a great pine tree, in the depths of the marsh country, lay stretched out flat upon a lofty limb of his home tree, intently watching a clumsy black figure which shuffled through the aisles of the pines far beneath him.

He thought the black, shadowy figure must be Moween, the black bear, but not feeling quite certain about it, Nemox peeked down over the limb curiously, hanging over as far as he dared, keeping his position upon the limb by digging his claws in deeply. His eyes sparkled maliciously and cunningly as he made sure that it actually was Moween herself. Then he knew she had come straight from her den up on Porcupine Ridge to forage for food, because down below, on the needle-strewn floor of the forest, Moween knew she could find plenty of prey for the taking. Close hidden beneath the low-hanging branches of the spruce bush, she sometimes came across a frightened partridge, and the roots of the pines were simply riddled with rabbit burrows. One might always rout out a sleepy hedgehog or two, if there chanced to be nothing better, for Moween knew the secret of avoiding its terrible quills and searching out the creature's weak spot, without injury to her own snout. So while Moween rummaged about, waddling in and out among the bushes, snuffing and grunting as she threw over a rotting log with her great, padded foot, Nemox, the crafty one, continued to watch her and think deeply. Very well he knew that the old mother bear had left her two innocent, furry little cubs back in her den, up on the side of the mountain. Nemox, the fisher, in one of his cat-like rambles, had run across them one day, just outside their door, cuffing each other about, and rolling over each other like kittens, as their mother watched them fondly. Well Nemox knew that the two cubs were still too young to follow their mother long distances, or down the steep ledges, so of course, he reasoned, they must be at home, alone and unprotected, this very minute.

Instantly Nemox had made his plans, and while the little black mother bear had buried her whole head in a hollow log, hoping to find honey, Nemox began to slide and claw himself down out of the pine tree, being careful, of course, to climb down upon the far side that Moween should not spy him. Then, like a fleet shadow, he slipped off through the thick underbrush, and following the wide swath of the mother bear's trail, he set out for her den.

Everybody knows that Nemox, the fisher, is the craftiest, most savage and powerful fighter of his age in the marshes, and most of his kindred feared him, giving him a wide berth. Nemox belonged to the cat family, and was sometimes called "the black cat of the woods." Sinuous of body and not unlike his cousin the weasel, only larger, he could readily leap forty or fifty feet, and always landed, cat-like, upon his prey. To all this was added great knowledge of woodcraft, and reasoning powers, for the clever fisher had easily studied out the fact that the bear had left her cubs unprotected. No wonder then that the fisher was reckoned as a terror of the marsh country, for it took the craftiest of the wild to outwit him.

In and out between the rocky ledges and tall ferns, always heading for the bear's den, traveled Nemox, and just as he drew near the spot where the little mother bear had cleverly hidden her den, he came right upon the little cubs, who were just outside the entrance of the den, and lay rolling over each other, having a regular frolic, cuffing at a swarm of black butterflies which fluttered about the milkweed blossoms. But the pretty sight of the round, furry babies of Moween at play did not for an instant touch the cruel heart of the fisher, who merely bared his sharp teeth as he hid behind a convenient blackberry bush watching them.

With twitching tail and whiskers, cat-like, the fisher began to creep stealthily toward his prey, flattening his lithe body and keeping out of sight as he crept nearer and nearer the innocent cubs. A swift dart, and he shot straight through the air and launched himself upon one of the cubs, while the other one sat up in amazement and began to whimper like a frightened child. Soon Nemox was busy with tooth and nail over the limp carcass of the cub, when suddenly his keen ear caught the sound of a stealthy pad, pad, pad; so light a footstep it was that no one but Nemox could have heard it. Instantly, fearing the return of the mother bear, Nemox left the wounded cub, for he had no notion of letting Moween, the angry mother, catch him at his cruel work, as well Nemox knew that with one blow of her great paw, armed with its lance-like claws, she could strike him to earth. He realized he would be no match for her unless he chanced to catch her napping.

So the fisher drew off, watching his chances from a safe distance, for, if the truth were known, Nemox was, in some respects, unless cornered, cowardly. He slunk into the shadow of a dark ledge, where his dark fur blended so well with the gloom that he remained completely concealed. He realized that he had taken himself off just in time, for the next instant the tall brakes were thrust aside; but instead of the mother bear making her appearance, who should peer out but Eelemos, the fox. Very cautiously the fox came forth from the bushes, and peered out in rather surprised fashion upon the scene before him; the badly wounded cub, and the other one, who still whimpered and whined helplessly, crying for its mother. Now the fox chanced to be very hungry, and the sight of the wounded cub tempted him. So he crept warily forward, his yellow eyes all agleam, and so intent was the fox upon the coming feast that he paid no attention to the other cub's little whine of joy and recognition as a great, black, furry bulk fairly tore its way through the thick jungle. Mad with rage and fear Moween's little red eyes flashed with anger as she caught sight of the fox and her wounded cub, and with one great bound she was upon him, growling terribly, and then, before the fox could even defend himself, the mother bear had laid him low, and soon all that remained of the proud, sly fox was just a battered red pelt, and a bedraggled, limp brush. Then Moween went back to attend to the little wounded cub, uttering low whines of distress, and lapping it tenderly, trying to revive it.

All this time, Nemox, the fisher, was peering out at her from a crack in the ledge, and he had seen the awful fate of Eelemos, the fox, and was very thankful he had got away from the den just in time. Now the fisher had not chanced to select the best spot for his hiding-place, for back inside of the ledge was the home of Unk-Wunk, the hedgehog, who had been asleep inside all the time, curled up in a round ball, until, finally, Nemox had so crowded him that he became impatient and suddenly unrolling himself, just to teach the intruder better manners, he gave him a smart slap across his sneaky pointed snout with his dreadful quilly tail. Nemox was so taken by surprise that, stifling his angry snarls so the mother bear might not hear him, he sneaked back home to the pine forest, his snout full of sharp quills, and spent most of the night spitting crossly and trying to pull them out of his burning flesh.

Next morning, bright and early, Nemox started off hunting once more. He climbed many trees looking for game, but in vain; he even found no partridges roosting down in lower branches, as usual, for already they had left their nightly haunts. At last Nemox reached the foot of a giant hackmatack tree, and right in the top of its branches he spied a great loose bundle of leaves and twigs.

"Ah," thought Nemox, "the hawks have a young family up there, or possibly there are eggs in the nest; so much the better," for Nemox loved eggs almost more than a young hawk. Very hungry was Nemox by this time, so he began to climb the tree. At last he reached a limb where he could peer into the nest. He was thankful that the old hawks were away, for there were eggs in the nest. Nemox knew he must hasten, for a brooding hawk is never long away from her eggs. Flattening himself close to the limb Nemox crawled to it, and had just sampled one egg, when with a sudden, wild rush of whirling wings, the mother hawk landed right upon his back, digging her sharp talons into his quivering flesh, as he snarled and spit and tore in her grasp. Finally, with a swift twist of his agile body, Nemox managed to reach the throat of the hawk, and in spite of the beating wings, which nearly thrashed the breath from his body, Nemox clung and clung to the hawk's throat, until they both fell to earth. And then Nemox had his first decent meal in days, and afterward he climbed up to the nest and finished off the eggs, which he did not forget.

Now high above the nest of the hawk, and over toward the lake, stood a lonely hemlock tree, its limbs broken off by storm after storm. Upon the summit of this tree Quoskh, the great blue heron, came year after year to build her nest and raise her brood. From her high nest, where she sat brooding the young herons, now just out of their pin-feather age, the mother heron could plainly look down upon her neighbor the hawk, and saw all the terrible tragedy which took place. She saw the dark, slim body of Nemox, the robber of the marshes, as he battled with the mother hawk, and then the end of it all. Quoskh, the heron, was afraid for her own young, so much so that for a long while afterward she dreaded to leave them alone long enough to fly off after food. Soon, however, they became large enough to fly to the lake with her, and she was glad. But Quoskh never forgot about the hateful fisher, and always hoped that some day she might get the best of him.

Right in the heart of the marsh-land lay Black Lake. Spread out like a sheet of molten lead it lay, its lonely waters walled about by thick jungles of sedge and cattails; a desolate spot, seldom visited by man, but known and haunted by all the kindred of the wild. You might trace their well-worn trails through the swamp on all sides. Here came Moween, the black bear, and her one cub, for the other she had lost. The sharp teeth of Nemox had done their work. On the edge of the lake Unk-Wunk, the porcupine, loved to loaf, digging out lily roots, and toward night, when shadows crept over the water, Nemox, the fisher, would sneak down, hoping to trap some little wild thing.

One day about twilight, when the little herons were half-grown, a large colony of herons came to the lake. It was approaching time for their annual colonizing plans, and they always meet and talk it over. Down they flocked in droves, on wide azure wings, calling to each other their lonely salute, "Quoskh, quoskh." And after standing on the pebbly shore solemnly upon one foot, for a while, at a signal they all began to dance a most fantastic sort of a dance, which is called "the heron dance." Many were the curious eyes watching the strange dance of the herons. Among them was Nemox, the fisher, who almost forgot to hide himself, so taken up in watching the herons was he. However, as he watched them a sudden, fascinating odor came to his nostrils, and he forgot everything else—it was catnip.

Soon he reached the bed of catnip, all silvery green leaves, sparkling with dew. He nibbled and ate, until finally, overcome completely by the fascinating odor, he simply lay down and rolled about, purring like a cat for sheer delight. He felt dreamy and care-free. But just as he was enjoying himself supremely, down floated the wide wings of Quoskh, the great blue heron, and with two stabs of her sword-like beak she had blinded Nemox, and with her wings beaten the breath completely out of his body.

Then, triumphantly, the heron spread her great blue wings and flew off into the twilight, calling "quoskh, quoskh, quoskh" to her mate across the silence of the marshes.

XXIV

THE KEEPER OF TAMARACK RIDGE

SOLOMON of old was wise and old in years. So too was Solomon, the old gray lynx, the keeper of Tamarack Ridge. Crafty and cruel too was this Solomon, and feared and dreaded by most of his wild neighbors on the ridge, and also by all the dwellers of the swamp below the ridge.

Solomon's thick coat was hoary, of a yellowish brown, and mottled and shabby, and his large round head terminated in sharp, pointed ears, set off by coarse, tassel-like tufts of black hair, which gave him a sly, sinister expression. Although Solomon the lynx was half the size of a full-grown panther, he could creep through the forest so silently that the soft pad, pad of his feet upon the soft mosses, and the time of his passing was known to few. He never extended any polite courtesies to anything he met, for his disposition was so ugly and mean that should he chance to meet a bobcat or a porcupine, he would always bare his cruel teeth in an ugly snarl, and slink away into the shadows. He mated with none but his own family, two interesting kitten cubs, and their mother.

Solomon Lynx was the oldest and almost the last one left of his tribe in the section of Tamarack Ridge. Once they were plentiful enough in the Canadian forests, but they had all disappeared, leaving only Solomon and his family as keeper of the ridge. Each year he and his wild mate raised their family there. Half-way up the side of the mountain lay the ridge, one of the wildest places in that section, covered over by a thick growth of tamarack and mountain hemlocks. At the foot of the ridge, scooped out in a basin between the mountains, lay a small, deep lake, and beyond the lake is Balsam Swamp.

To the small lake the boys come occasionally to fish for trout or catfish, and here, when the deer laws are off, come hunters from afar. Excepting for these rare intrusions, Tamarack Ridge, the lake, and Balsam Swamp, are inhabited only by the wild dwellers of the forest, creatures of feathers and fur.

The den of Solomon the lynx lay concealed in the thick tamaracks, beneath a jutting ledge of rock, the remains of an abandoned lime quarry. Their den was not a pleasant spot; just a deep, dark hole, which runs far under the ledge, from the entrance of which often peered forth Solomon's crafty face, lighted with yellow eyes which flashed fire upon dark nights. The floor of the den was strewn over with bones, the remains of cruel, snarling feasts, when the whole family fought over the possession of a carcass. Sometimes it would be a young rabbit, a raccoon, or some other timid little wood neighbor, and most of them knew the place of Solomon's den, and always made a wide détour when possible, not caring to cross his path; so he remained absolute monarch of the ridge.

One day, late in fall, two village boys came into the swamp to set snares for muskrats. They knew about the keeper of Tamarack Ridge and his evil reputation. For often his horrid yell might be heard on the outskirts of the village on moonlight nights, and they knew the lynx was abroad. And sometimes, if hard pressed, Solomon was overbold, and he and his mate even ventured out of the swamp, and carried off lambs from the farmyards, and once even a young calf. So that finally the farmers offered a bounty to any one who would put an end to the old lynx. So the boys had brought along a large steel trap with them, weighing about eighty pounds, strong enough to hold any lynx once he was caught in its great steel teeth. But when the boys came to set the trap they discovered, to their dismay, that some of the steel teeth were so badly worn off that the trap could not be made to catch properly. Finally by stuffing beneath the plate some leaves, they raised it enough to make the teeth meet, and then baiting their trap with a fresh sheep's head, they hastened away, for it was by that time nearly dark, and they were afraid that the old lynx might even then have been watching them, and might leap down upon them from some overhanging tree, as he had a way of doing when it suited him.

To tell the truth, Solomon had seen the boys, and his curiosity had been aroused as to just what they had been about down on the edge of the lake. From his place of concealment, lying out flat upon the lime ledge just above his den, he had watched and peered at them between the overhanging tamaracks. And then as the boys started to leave, just as a pleasant warning to them, that they might not approach the ridge, he raised his head and sent out, one after another, a series of his blood-curdling, horrid yells, which so terrified the boys that they took to their heels and ran, as fast as they were able, away, away from those awful cries.

That night it was clear and keen, with frost in the air and young ice in the lowlands, so that when Solomon at last leisurely took his way down from the ridge, with strong, sure leaps, he finally came to where the trap was set, and by this time bait, trap, and all were frozen solid. So Solomon had no difficulty about the trap; it could not spring, and he devoured the bait unharmed, tossing the trap far aside in contempt when he had secured the sheep's head.

As you can well imagine, the boys, when they dared come back to see if their trap had been sprung, and if they had actually caught a lynx, were thoroughly disgusted at the outcome of their well-laid plans, and almost gave up all hope of ever capturing the lynx. All through the winter months, after snowfall, Solomon's tracks might be found, as they were readily distinguished from those of the foxes and other wild things because Solomon always took long, flying leaps across the snow, leaving a set of deep, round holes wherever his tufted feet struck. More than once his awful yell had been heard upon moonlight nights close to the traveled roads, and many were afraid to venture out late at night because of the lynx, and the little children would whimper and cry, and hide their heads in terror beneath the quilts, when they heard Solomon's screech in the night.

When early spring came, the boys came again to the lake, this time for the mountain trout, which were running well. They came with a team, intending to camp in the balsams all night, and tethered their horse securely between two rocks, tying him with a double halter that he might not stray. The fish were biting splendidly along about twilight, and the boys were out on a raft some distance from shore. They carried a lantern with a reflector to attract the fish, and were having great sport. They thought about the lynx, but the sport was so keen that they forgot their fears. The trout would make a circuit of the round lake traveling in schools, and when a school of fish came their way, the boys were kept busy with their lines, hauling in trout. Then they would wait idly until the next school came around. During these periods of inactivity the boys were quiet, and a deep stillness settled over everything. Once a loon screeched, and then regularly, over in Balsam Swamp, commenced the old hoot owl's lonely cry, "Waugh, waugh, waugh, hu, hu-hu, hu," and then an old settler or a bullfrog "zoom, zoom'd," over in the marshes.

Then all at once, in the awful stillness which had settled over the lake, came a crashing sound in the spruce bush along shore, close to where the boys had tethered their horse, followed by the well-known, awful yell of the lynx.

"It's after the horse, perhaps," suggested one of the boys. Awful thought; they must pull to shore and find out. So, in spite of their own terror, they poled ashore, and when they reached the spot where their horse had been tied he was no longer there, for the animal, terrified out of its senses by the near-by yell of Solomon, had broken his halters and made off. The boys decided then and there that they did not care to remain over night, so one of them took the wagon shafts, while the other boy pushed behind, and they tore down the road toward the village. Half-way down the mountain road they came across their frightened horse, and, minus their fish, finally reached home.

Thus did Solomon hold the fort, and remain on as undisputed keeper of the ridge. Never could he be trapped or shot, until finally the patience of the farmers was at an end, and they resolved to rally and have a grand hunt for the lynx family; but even then they failed to catch him, and this is how it happened.

One night that fall, Solomon and his family had been out upon one of their bold raids. Right into a farmer's barn-yard Solomon ventured this time, while his mate waited for him farther up the trail. When he met her he dragged after him a fine, fat sheep, and together they made their way to the den to share the great feast with the waiting cubs. When it was finished, they all curled themselves up for a long, gluttonous sleep, which would last probably until their pressing hunger again awakened them.

Gradually a brooding silence settled over mountain and swamp. The moon was setting and hung, a slim crescent, just over the edge of the dark spruces. Always, before dawn, there comes a hush, when even the owls and frogs are quiet, and the hermit thrush has finished her all night lullaby. It is as if all Nature waited; waited for the birth of a new day.

Then down from the lime ledge, just above Solomon's den, slipped a dark, lithe figure, slim, with small, sinister eyes; it half-scrambled, half-clawed its way down to a level with the den of the lynx. It moved leisurely but surely, in and out among the tall, rank ferns, threading its way with unerring scent, the scent being fresh meat. Like a shadow, the long, slim body stole inside the bone-strewn den of the lynx, nosing about among the gnawed, discarded bones of the sheep in disdain, and uttering a hissing, baffled growl of disappointment.

Suddenly a low, rumbling growl of warning came from the half-awakened lynx, who had somehow scented the presence of an intruder in the den, but the growl did not frighten off the small, slim visitor, who must be very brave indeed to face Solomon. The eyes of the lynx, mere slits of sleepiness, gradually opened wider and wider. He had caught sight of the stranger, and now thoroughly awake he bared his teeth in an ugly snarl of rage at being disturbed from his slumbers.

The next instant, like a flash of lightning, before Solomon knew how to prepare himself for attack, the slim, dark body had sprung straight for his throat. In vain the lynx shook and scratched and turned himself about. He could not rid himself of the small dark body which had fastened itself in his throat and clung and clung. Gradually the eyes of Solomon lost all luster, and he sank back limp and dead. While all this had been going on the mother lynx and her cubs had awakened, and the old lynx, intent only upon saving the cubs, had stolen off like a shadow, the cubs following her, into the darkness. They had deliberately deserted Solomon in his extremity. Off over the mountain the old lynx led the cubs, and did not stop until she had hidden them in a safe retreat miles away, upon another spur of the mountain, and she never ventured back to Tamarack Ridge again.

When the hunters found the lynx den, they also found all that remained of Solomon lying cold and stark in the edge of the den. And one of the men remarked:

"Only a weasel could do that. The lynx met his match that time."

Thus ended the long, terrifying reign of Solomon the lynx, and the den beneath the dark, overhanging boughs of the tamarack is now without its keeper.